LAST NOTES FROM A SPLIT PENINSULA

Poems and Prose Poems

by
Robert Perchan

UnCollected Press

LAST NOTES FROM A SPLIT PENINSULA
Copyright © 2021 by Robert Perchan

All rights reserved. This book in full form may not be used or reproduced by electronic or mechanical means without permission in writing from the author and UnCollected Press.

Cover Art:
Dan-o Day Scene
Shin Yun-bok (1758 – 1813)
28.2 cm x 35.6 cm watercolor on paper

Back Cover Photo by Mi-kyung Lee

Book Design by:

UnCollected Press
8320 Main Street, 2nd Floor
Ellicott City, MD 21043

For more books by UnCollected Press:
www.therawartreview.com

First Edition 2020
ISBN: 978-1-7360098-9-5

For Kenneth May

CONTENTS

NOTES FROM A SPLIT PENINSULA 1
    SARGE: BY WAY OF INTRODUCTION 2
    SPLICE OF LIFE: DALDONGNEH, PUSAN 5
    DRILL 7
    A VISITOR 8
    A GLIMPSE OF 9
    OR SO THE GRIM GERMAN WOULD HAVE US BELIEVE 10
    BACHELOR STRIPPED BARE BY HIS HOUSEWIVES, EVEN 11
    ON BUMPING INTO A FORMERLY SNAGGLE-TOOTHED YOUNG NEIGHBOR 12
    4:40 A.M. ANONYMOUS PHONE CALL 13
    KOREAN ROCK GARDEN 14
    ESL TEACHER 15
    MISS MIN'S MAGIC MONDAY MORNING 16
    PER SPECULUM ET IN AENIGMATE 18
    IN ENGLISH THE KOREAN WORD *BOP* MEANS "GLUTINOUS RICE;" OR, AT THE WOMEN'S COLLEGE 19
    CONSOLATION 21
    MY FIRST AND LAST COUNTESS: AT THE WORLD CONGRESS OF POETS, SEOUL, SOUTH KOREA 23
    DIVINATIONS 26
    INTRODUCTION TO UNIVERSAL PSYCHOPHONETICS: THE B's 28

KOREAN LANGUAGE IDIOMS LESSON #307 29
PUSAN RAINDROP PUSAN WOMAN: FOR THE GIRLS OF TEXAS STREET 30
SIMILIA SIMILIBUS CURANTUR, CANICULA 32
BARBERSHOP SEX: AN INITIATION 33
ON HIS FABLED GENEROSITY; OR, HER AMERICAN DREAM 34
RECOVERY 36
POETRY TOO HAS ITS ROLE TO PLAY, HE INSISTED 37
ZEN DETECTIVE EXAM QUESTION #38 39
EXPRESSWAY BHIKKHU 40
SIX FOOTNOTES TO THE BUDDHA'S BIRTHDAY 41
THE GENTLE MONK: A FIRE SERMON 43
A TALE OF TWO PENINSULAS 44
IN A STATION OF THE METRO 45
HAIBUN EPILOGUE 46
DOWN LETTER HOME TO A POET FRIEND 47
AN ANGEL OF ENGLISH 48
RECOGNITION 50

B'S CHOREA: A POET'S JOURNAL 51

MUSING MISS KIM 96
ART 97
DOMESTICITY 98
TECHNIQUE 100
ORPHODONTIA 101
CLASS 103

CHINOISERIE	104
PEN(W(O))MANSHIP	105
DEREGULATION	106
TRANSPARENCE	107
IDENTITY	108
INTEGRATION	109
GILLAGAIN	111
CLOSURE	112
FATE	113
STYLE	114
IMMORTALITY	115
LAMIA	117
SIN	119
ARDOR	120
COMPETITION	121
DECONSTRUCTION	123
AMNESIS	124
TIME	125
PROPINQUITY	126
LOSS	127
TRUTH	128

NOTES FROM A SPLIT PENINSULA

SARGE: BY WAY OF INTRODUCTION

About a week before I was to rendezvous in
South Korea for my first full time teaching
job on dry land, I sat in the lounge of Manila's
Admiral Hotel waiting for the night to fall.
The burly U.S. Marine eighteen-year-man
sergeant who bellied up to the bar alongside
me and bought a round had a serpentine
latticework of tattoos that slithered from
his wrists up under the mat of hair on his
arms and disappeared into his shirtsleeves.
*Say you're goin' to Koh-REE-ah? Man,
them little Koh-REE-ahn bastards is tough.
In Nam the U.S. Marines wasn't afraid of
no suckers. 'Ceptin' those little Kor-REE-ahn
Marines bastards—and they was on* our *side!
Man, I seed a platoon of they's guys lined
up at attention for inspection one mornin'.
Cap'n walks down the line tappin' each one
of 'em in the balls with a whip handle sort
of approval-like. Not hard. But by no means
gentle. I wouldn't fancy it. Then he comes
to one guy—a big sucker—and the cap'n
looks down at the poor feller's crotch and
barks somethin' in they's lingo. Turns out
the poor fucker had his cock and balls on
the wrong side of his trouser seam. Before
you could say jake the guy was on the ground
in a heap bleedin' from every pore on his
body. I never seed a man reduced to mush
so fast. 'Ceptin' in combat, of course. Them
was the Koh-REE-ahn Marines. Tough.*
I took a slow, silent pull on my San Miguel.

But they's women's all right. Pretty. Just don't cross one. Just don't cross one. One of they's gals prett' near tore me a new one one night just for dancin' in another club time I was posted there. Territorial, that's what I calls they's gals. Territorial. Sounds like a pretty tough crowd, I said. *You bet. Gotta be. With they's frozen DMZ and them crazy fuckers up north of that.* Sarge looked down at my duffel bag with its USS DECATUR stenciled on the side. *You Navy?* he inquired. *You don't look Navy. Navy don't allow a haircut like 'at these days.* Civilian, I explained, stammering a little, flushing at the wimpishness and absurdity of what I did for a living in the presence of a Man of War. A teacher, I said. PACE. Program for Afloat College Education. *Yeh? I heard of you's guys. Teachin' on the ships.* I teach English. *Yeh. I heard of that.* Composition. Literature. Rhetoric. *Well, I don't know about that.* For sailors who are interested. With a little time on their hands. College credits. Those Westpac cruises can last eight or nine months. Not much else to do. Study. *Navy's okay,* Sarge allowed. *But I wouldn't want to spend a whole military career walkin' around with a cork stuck up my butthole. Nope. No thanks. Not me.* I sprang for another round and expeditiously tossed mine down and made my way out the Admiral's

plastic-vine-covered arbor with the EXIT
sign above it, eager for the frissons of
unfamiliar ways and volatile women and
a real job on dry land but couldn't help
wondering which side of my crotch seam
I should start packing my junk on.

SPLICE OF LIFE: DALDONGNEH, PUSAN

The neighborhood housewives
step out of their concrete bunker homes
wedged in the urban mountainside
to carry on their gossipy quarrels
(*"She said I said you said she* SAID WHAT?*"*)
right outside my open kitchen window
like the concrete ramp out there
is a stage
and ever since the World Cup
everybody in this country thinks it's Showtime.
A baggy pants old man
who backed a truck over his only schoolboy son
some thirty years ago
(so people tell me)
walks down the mountain backwards
every afternoon
three steps at a time
stops
sets down
a mysterious canvas satchel
turns his head
over his shoulder
checks the clearance
of his path
shouts something in grouchy Korean
(the neighborhood women answer back and yuck it up)
and lurches downward again
three more steps
in his eternal reverse.
Now and then a dolled up *agashi*
("Virgin Miss")
uneasy in her fashionable
and ill-fitting womanhood

passes with pursed lips and pinched dreams
of honeymoon sex and trousseaus.
Comfortable in my solitary kitchen
it's like watching a local tv soap
of passion, hope, loss and betrayal.
Until I remember how I heard
Korean farmwives interrupt
their bickering to curse
any male who trespasses on their
country kitchen sanctuary:
DON'T YOU COME DRAGGING
YOUR GOD DAMN TESTICLES
THROUGH HERE EVER AGAIN!

DRILL

This kid from down the block has
a way of wailing from spitefulness
or pain—you can't ever tell which—
that sounds like what you might
expect to come out of the barred
windows of a lunatic asylum: it
starts low and builds with a slow
fury until the whole neighborhood
cringes. Then quite unaccountably
the kid shuts up. Just like that.
Air-raid over. No bombs fallen.
The kid is watching something—
dog, cat, pigeon, motorcycle—
from a world of panic to rapture
he rocks back and forth while
the rest of us scan the empty skies.

A VISITOR

The doorbell rings and I traipse across the room
to answer it, expecting *X* and the pricey bottle
of mulberry mushroom rice wine she promised.
But framed in the doorway is a young man in
a white t-shirt with rolled up sleeves and spanking
new army camouflage workpants. He sports
a post-adolescent fringe moustache that one
associates with unpredictable hormone surges
and teen-age street corner menace.
                              "BUG,"
he announces shrilly. "DIE!"
                              Were this a story
of criminal mayhem and gang revenge he would
no doubt lift a shiv to my belly and plunge it in.
Instead he politely allows himself into the flat
and commences to spray the baseboards under my
kitchen sink with a small brass nozzle attached
to a plastic jug of insecticide strapped to his waist.
"Sorry," he smiles shyly and shrugs. "No English."

A GLIMPSE OF

a spastic
schoolboy satchel
strapped to
his back
elbows wrists
shoulders and
blades his
"angles"
pumping and
jerking with
the randomness
of ping pong
balls
in a lottery
hopper

is suddenly
transformed

Duchamp maybe

into the mad
dance
of electrons
around
the source of
all wonder

OR SO THE GRIM GERMAN WOULD HAVE US BELIEVE

On the nights he comes home late
from the Goethe Institute
to their apartment across the hall
he stops at the door and clears
his throat – loud – like a post-horn
blown before a castle portcullis.
This is to announce he's not
the neighborhood rapist. It's
him. The Grim German. Come home.
Inside, his powdered Korean wife
has pushed their potted Black Forest
into place. His woodcutter's ax
leans up against his chair.
Quietly he enters. Smells wolf:
a long table spread with meat
and bread and beer. He eats.
Wipes his woodcutter's sleeve
across his woodcutter's chops.
Whiffs his fur. Yawns the cavernous
yawn of muzzles. Drops down
on all fours. Catches the bedroom
scent. Closes. Nuzzles a cold
black Teutonic nose into a pale
comose Korean rose. Or so
the Grim German would have us believe.

BACHELOR STRIPPED BARE
BY HIS HOUSEWIVES, EVEN

I push my wobbly shopping cart
along the supermarket aisle.
The nosey Korean housewives
crane their necks and peer
down into the wire basket
as if the meager contents there
(two cantaloupes, bacon, beer)
might reveal the real secret
of my Otherness: So this, I
decide, is what it must be like
to have big tits, a plunging neckline
and nowhere to hide.

ON BUMPING INTO A FORMERLY SNAGGLE-TOOTHED YOUNG NEIGHBOR

Why do girls with
braces on their teeth
always look so much
like cats when they
smile? Even their ears
appear more pointed
and alert. Their cheek
bones higher and their
eyes so calculating
and fixed. When they
flare their nostrils
you can almost see
the whiskers twitch.
Maybe it's just all
that metal-work
against the tender
pink of gums—that
complication of
wires and brackets
and tiny hooks
between their lips:
that hint of bird
cage door, mouse
trap sprung.

4:40 A.M. ANONYMOUS PHONE CALL

At first I thought the whisper
was a witch's
scorched female rasp.
It said she was underneath a blanket
her father asleep in the other room
and strict. It said she had
"a yellow streak." I tried to place
the idiom: schoolteacher, student, nurse? Any
could know it. A Pusan twang: like a guitar
string snapping in the middle of a chord.
And then the sex started. It said
imagine my breast. I said your
nipple is between my teeth. Touch
your clit. Rub. (She: "Lub?" & I: "No. Rub.
R-u-b.") Which she did. Or must've
for then the breathing, heavier
like a dry wind trapped inside a can:
the Phone. She came. The voice
at war with submission, choked
on itself. "My God! There's a light
on! He's up! Did I make
so much noise?"
"It's okay."
"You sure?"
"Yes."
And then she started in again,
without me. The wind fiercer now
trapped inside that can. Crackle.
Silence. The line
dead in my gone dead hand.

**KOREAN
ROCK
GARDEN**

In May
the white
pepper gas
flower
blooms
on campus,
the dung green
soldiery
its rich
compost:
the angry
students
buzz in and
out
gathering
the hot
pollen
to carry
back
to their hives
of burning
eyes
and blind
golden
honey
of change

ESL TEACHER

"**brogue** n̲ [perh. fr. IrGael *barrog* wrestling hold; fr. the idea that unfamiliar features of pronunciation must be the result of a physical impediment of the tongue]"

The English syllables clung like polyps to the lining of their throats, intractable. He fed them razor blades. Their tongues thrashed madly against the enamel of their teeth. He served them up bridles and whips and reins. l's grappled with r's and refused to let go the stlangrehord. He packed their mouths with referees. Fat mustachioed ones, like cotton wadding. Lips bounced open when they should have stayed shut, stuck tight when they should have parted, just so. He piled high a plate with oiled hinges and snap-locks, and shoveled them in. Gradually the mouthparts fell in synch, cam bone and lever tendon and piston muscle. Correct pronunciation! And now, he thought, for the trickiest lesson of all. Proper intonation.
    And attached the electrodes.
    He would save the unguents and salves for later,
Level 2: The Compliant Pushovers.

MISS MIN'S MAGIC MONDAY MORNING

2,000,000 years into human evolution,
Deok-hee "Ducky" Min of Pusan, South Korea,
discovers, while toweling off after a hot shower,
that the *Homo sapiens* nose is detachable.
A soft click, at first, right between her cheeks
where bone locks into bone to form her face.
Then a slight sucking sound as the nose
pulls away from its tender bed of pink flesh.
She stares at it a moment, nestled in the folds
of her towel. Turns it over with the awe
and fascination of a mother's wonderment
at the precious appendages of her neonate.
The flared nares. The celestial upturned slope
ending in a tip a little more pointed than
she would have expected. The tiny mole
on the left side. Gingerly she lifts it up
to the center of her face and with a nudge
of her thumb clicks it back in place again.
Alone in the world with this delicious
new knowledge, on the cross-town bus
to campus she sees herself on a tv talk show,
passing her nose around an astonished panel
of movie stars, pop singers and fashion models.
Later a personal interview with the new lady
President of the Republic. A rare private
audience with the Dalai Lama. An envoy
from Secretary-General of the UN
Ban Ki-moon inviting her to assume
the throne as Empress of the Universe.
Even dispatched on a Delicate Mission
of Peace to that Supreme Leader—pudgy,

murderous, nose-thumbing Kim Jong Un.
Or, better, a secret to be kept and shared
only with that special someone—yours truly,
the humble spinner of this fantastic yarn.

PER SPECULUM ET IN AENIGMATE

Sometime during
the windy night
the pigeon either
flew or was blown
into the filmy
unwashed pane
of the fourteenth
floor classroom
window and left
the splayed and
stunned impression
of sudden death
on the wing in
a morning sun
that revealed how
shit happens to
the least of things
just that moment
you least expect it
as my students
glide in with their
notebooks and pens
inquisitive eyes
insouciant smiles
and preening in
tiny mirrors their
immaculate and
buoyant plumage

IN ENGLISH THE KOREAN WORD *BOP* MEANS "GLUTINOUS RICE;" OR, AT THE WOMEN'S COLLEGE

> *Can't stop messin'*
> *with the danger zone*
>   — Cyndi Lauper

Halfway through the semester
finally
they stop asking me
How old are you?
Is it true you're not married?
How much do you drink?
Don't you miss your hometown?
And we go on
to deeper things
What, sir, does
she-bop mean?
Good question
I wouldn't've known
except I read
Rolling Stone
to keep up with
the scene back home
It means, I say
authoritatively
Female Autoeroticism
Blank stares all around
exotic frogs
on lotus pads
gazing up
into the Light
so I say it

in Korean
yoja jah-wee haeng-wee
and I sense a ripple
in this placid pond
of peninsular souls
How does he know
that bad word?
they whisper
quite rightly
given my struggles
with their tongue
but at least I've
let them know
what we sing about
back where I come from

CONSOLATION

*A Chicken Walked
Through It With
Boots On* my male
soon to graduate
students recall
in their jocular
reminiscences of
mess hall banter
the watery and
tasteless broth
they were ladled
for the two years
of conscription
they served as
ROK field grunts
which well may
help to explain
the near ubiquity
of cheap fried
chicken joints on
this peninsula
with salaries
stagnant and all
the plum jobs
going to grads of
the elite schools:
no matter how
bad off you are
today in your
desperate search
for work there is

just almost about
enough money
in your pocket
to feed an army

MY FIRST AND LAST COUNTESS: AT THE WORLD CONGRESS OF POETS, SEOUL, SOUTH KOREA

for Paola Lucarini Poggi

I kissed the hand of a countess once
at a poetry celebration in Seoul
when Andrei Vosnesenky recited
that Pablo Neruda poem about socks
as we sat at the round banquet tables
and she stared at me over the floral
centerpiece all evening long until
the food and the poetry were over
and a dapper gentleman in a blazer
who could have just stepped out
of an *Esquire* spread or Browning
monologue led the forty-eightish
contessa up to me and explained
that she did not speak English
but swore that mine was the very
face of her dear dead *papa* and so
was why she couldn't take her
eyes off of me and she hoped
she had not been rude or made
me otherwise uncomfortable
as in that instant she lifted
her hand ever so slightly and I
took it in my own and lifted it
ever so slightly to my lips as if
I had done it a thousand times
on such occasions and kissed
it drily just a touch really like
you see in the movies of *Anna
Karenina* or gatherings at Bath

in Jane Austen's *Persuasion*
and she smiled pleased as punch
and withdrew with her companion
as I myself withdrew to a lift
where I bumped into a dour Allen
Ginsberg who had been slammed
in the Korean newspapers after
visiting political dissidents in jail
upon his arrival on the peninsula
before shaking hands with those
dignitaries who had invited him
in the first place and so an insult
if you know anything about Asia
and said graceless ingrate guest
and so-called "Beatnik Poet"
had furthermore been informed
by a critic of some stature
in the nation's literary circles
via a stricken and abashed
young simultaneous interpreter
at a symposium on the day before
the banquet gala that the author
of "Howl" and "Sunflower Sutra"
knew not squat about The East
nor jack of True Buddhahood
and we all looked down at our feet
or fiddled with our headphones
and waited for it to be over and done
when AG lifted up his harmonium
and played something godawful

ugly or godawfully transcendental
dependent of course on your religion
Daoist Maoist Nirvanist Confucian
as somewhere in the auditorium
a countess who had seen better days
and wouldn't meet me till the next
for that docile lifting to the lips
sat staring at a stranger wearing
the face of a father she'd adored

DIVINATIONS

Once a year my good friend Yum gets a kick
out of afflicting the squeamish Westerner
in me with a free meal of *yang-gop-chang*:
a butane-fueled camp stove sits in the center
of a low table. On it is placed a square cast-iron
platen covered with crisp bright cooking foil.
The waitress adjusts the flame underneath and
with a pair of tongs lifts the beef tripe and cow
intestine from a wide platter and settles them on
the hot foil. After they've had the chance to sizzle
for a while, she lifts a pair of giant scissors and
with the confidence and aplomb of an accomplished
abdominal surgeon snips them into bite-sized
pieces. My reluctant chopsticks nudge a few of
these Night of the Living Dead morsels around
the platen until they are tender and browned.

Thus our ancient haruspex ancestors at their pagan
Stonehenge altars probed the entrails of slaughtered
and sacrificed goats and sheep and assorted bovines
to prophesy the success of a group hunt, the chance
of rain or advent of pestilence or plague or a Savior.

And thus my latest cancer screening with Dr. Kim,
the pert and affable resident in gastroenterology on
whom I've nursed a secret geezer crush for a month
now and frantically hope to make a good impression.
She taps the computer monitor on her desk with
a pencil as I peer over her shoulder at the moving
pictures of my colonoscopy results: *You had two
polyps,* she announces with characteristic gravitas
and triumph, *which we resected without nicking
the intestinal wall. They proved to be benign. This,*

however, she winces and points to a bean-shaped phantom on the screen, *is a rogue piece of fecal matter which you failed to eliminate beforehand.*

Thus assigned my proper station in precise Dr. Kim's hierarchy of ineptitudes, I skulk out her office door.

And thus later along the concrete Haeundae beach boardwalk I take a seat opposite an old coot fortune teller and for a Korean sawbuck he consults his books and charts cluttered with the strokes and slashes of Sino-Korean ideograms and gamboling Chinese zodiac critters. After a few moments' immersion in such Eastern arcana, he slides the Korean sawbuck back to me across his little table and indicates with a silent, knowing nod as much as to say: *No fortune today, pal. You got enough crap on your plate as it is.*

INTRODUCTION TO UNIVERSAL PSYCHOPHONETICS: THE B's

In the classic American film *One Flew Over the Cuckoo's Nest* virginal Billy Bibbit introduces himself to Jack McMurphy Nicholson with a stammer: B-b-billy B-b-bibbit. We, of course, are expected to recall that other innocent stammering victim of cruel authoritarian oppression, Herman Melville's B-b-billy B-b-budd. In Spanish *Juan Bobo* is a generic term for simpleton. In Puerto Rico, for example, the bubbly, gussied-up blubber boat with the huge bazoombies whom the neighborhood dullard takes to the Saturday night movies is known as *La Puerca de Juan Bobo*. Boob. Fool. In English, as you will learn, boob connects up with bosom, busty, buxom. With dumb blonde. Note how in "dumb" the final b is silent, yet perfectly at home there for all that, like the stuttering Babette of the ample bubbies in your high school class who always stood last in lunch line and never uttered a complete word. (Nevertheless, let me caution you at this point against ranging too far afield. Those males among you who have yet to make the trek to Brittany's Brest in France are in for a sore disappointment.) I understand that here in Korea, this land of yours to which I have, for all practical purposes, been exiled, girls with big breasts are also said to be proverbial dumbbells. No blondes over here, though. But, as you all know, the Korean word for fool is *bah-bo*. For a child's innocent smacking buss, *bo-bo*. Innocuous glutinous rice, a round bowl of which is taken at virtually every meal and which fills each mouth with gooey white stickiness, is called *bop*. And class, just to let you know what kind of guy I am, my given name is Robert, but my friends call me Bob. I think you now understand how I intend to teach this course, what will be expected of you this term, and what kind of bimbos I prefer.

KOREAN LANGUAGE IDIOMS LESSON #307

Fried Eggs, Koreans call them:
breasts of a flat-chested woman

reclining on her back to receive
her new honeymoon husband's

sigh of relief: *At least they're not
Two Wads of Gum on the Asphalt.*

PUSAN RAINDROP PUSAN WOMAN: FOR THE GIRLS OF TEXAS STREET

1

A tear wrung
from an ionized
thunderhead
gray as
a washrag
runs down along
the rib of
my umbrella
trembles for
a moment
the only
moment
it will ever
be called
beautiful
and drops
to the asphalt
where it joins
the green oil &
splintered glass
& gritty
perfunctory
kisses
of bootsoles

2

Get a grip, Poet
& get real

Be concrete &
listen: sidewalk
heel clack &
skirt swish &
streetwalker
sweet talk of
hard women
Their eyestalks
stalk our wads
& surround
our flesh suits
of appetite
that can't be
stripped off
Surround our
i, there's the rub

3

The one you
drag back
from that
sleazy dive
who proceeds
to hide
every single
knife in
your kitchen
has just
told you
a keen slice
of her real
life story

SIMILIA SIMILIBUS CURANTUR, CANICULA

Like the ancient Romans
the old time Koreans too
held the folk belief that
if bitten by a rabid dog
you snatch a handful
of its hair, singe it and
apply the poultice to
the puncture so as to
salve and heal it and
not go mad mutt mad.
This morning, with X
run off to her suave
and oh so suasive
medical officer lover
on the U.S. Army base
in Seoul I pluck from
my shower drain grate
the dank tangle of pubes
she shed as she washed
me out of her life and
swirl them into the cup
of viscous *soju* I raise
solemnly and silent to
Past and Future Facing
Roman Janus and toss
down to our boogie
nights and my looming
matutinal woodies
and gag on my version
of the venerable Like
Cures Like: *A Pinch of
Fur off the Crotch of
the Cur that Bit You.*

BARBERSHOP SEX: AN INITIATION

> "The Ministry of Justice estimates of the 6,788 barbershops operating in Seoul, as many as 2,000 provide lewd services."
> *The Korea Herald (ca. 1990's)*

In the darkened cubicle
After the scissors
The shears
The razor to the nape
The shampoo and blow-dry

She brings you cleanly off

And you go back
To your hotel
Decide there's a poem in it

And then you remember
A thirty-year-old snapshot
Of you
Getting your first haircut
Your innocent mug wild with tears

And then you decide
There was nothing special in it
After all
Just another matter of growing up
And getting hard

ON HIS FABLED GENEROSITY; OR, HER AMERICAN DREAM

Out of loneliness he calls her up and she comes over. Even toward midnight it's too hot to finish their watery bourbon and cokes, so they make love. She comes a single excruciating time and they marvel at how that happens when they're not drunk. (In such heat it's like work, so they take pride in themselves that way too.) Then she hits him up for 200 dollars for her Chicken Sexer Institute tuition. She wants to get to the shores of America, where she's heard a Korean woman with a trained eye and a scosh of intuition can make herself a healthy pile separating little yellow male balls of fluff from little yellow female ones by peeking up their day-old, ambiguous behinds. For months he hasn't had the heart to tell her about the new German spectroscopy machines. After all, she's up to 630 chicks an hour with an accuracy rate of 85.7%, tops in her class. And it's still muggy enough that he can mutter non-committally and nod out.

In the morning he feels better, a small breeze coming in out of the east off the Sea of Japan. After a solitary cup of coffee, he nudges her bones around – she doesn't eat well, he knows – to get her up. It's fascinating to gaze down at her Asian maidenhair fern muff and muse upon the Transparent and the Veiled. He asks her if she had any dreams.

"Yes. But you know, they were all mixed up."

He smiles. As a poet, he knows all about it.

Then she: "Did you have any dreams?"

So he tells her about his weird one, neglecting to mention he has a variation on it once a month or so. "I dreamed I was back in college at Freshman Orientation but all the incoming coeds had little Hitler moustaches or long Sumerian beards. And I had lost my pants too. And nobody would help me find them."

"Oh thank you," she chirps, and wraps her arms around his neck. "I knew you would understand."

RECOVERY

After six weeks in Hell
I pull my claws
out of my eyes
look around
have written six poems
(that's one a week—though
we'll have to sit on these)
According to AFKN Radio
the Indians have won
five in a row
A check really was
in the mail
X will be on the train
down tomorrow
from Seoul
and if she isn't
(with her breasts that are
cyclones
in which my thoughts
fly apart)
I'm going to be able
to take it
Tight, man
the tough guys say
who know

**POETRY TOO HAS
ITS ROLE TO PLAY,
HE INSISTED**

The day after
typhoon Kong-Rey
slammed Pusan
I ramble through
the seaside park
above the beach
and smack into
a freshly spun
span of sticky
filaments strung
twig to naked twig.
Like the city crew
and hired on
day laborers
and high school
kid volunteers
down on the sand
picking up debris
and bagging it neatly
even the spiders
have to bust their
arachnid butts
reweaving storm
shredded webs
on a Sunday in
this workaholic
nation of salesclerks
factory hands
and office drones
to do their part
and get it all back

in ship-shape order.
Everyone save me
and the curious
wry necked woman
with the rictus grin
in her wheelchair
on the boardwalk
has a job to do
and pitches in.
I'm a foreigner
poet pen poised
for the next line
and so toil not
neither do I spin:
Still she sits regal
here in her chair
with the sea breeze
riffling her hair
and imperiously
observes the action
impervious to guilt
or so one presumes
but not to the urge
to dive right in and
gladly lend a hand
as she thinks, I'm sure:
That idler over there
taking it all in
with his precious
thoughts and specious
English words
be damned.

ZEN DETECTIVE
EXAM QUESTION #38

How long does it take
an abandoned black
Cadillac
sitting in the far
corner
of an empty parking
lot to start
reeking like
a murdered monk
if there is no one
around
to smell it?

EXPRESSWAY BHIKKHU

On his knees
a Buddhist monk
in gray robes
head bowed
arms outstretched
mendicant
palms cupped
dreams of
Nirvana:
a toll booth
coin basket

SIX FOOTNOTES TO THE BUDDHA'S BIRTHDAY

I

The fabled courtesans. Miss Kim sports no natural shag between her sleek thighs. Nowhere for Mr. Louse to hang his little black lantern of an egg. And on the Buddha's Birthday!

II

The Buddha and Jackie Gleason in *The Hustler*. Twin rotundities: East Egg and West Egg. A fat Buddha in gray robes tapping his pool cue on the floor. Not cigarette smoke but smoldering joss sticks bluing the air. One ball clacks against another. A single sound, complete in itself.

III

Would you believe Yum Bum-suck is a real Korean man's name? Miss Kim once told me that as a child her mother often scolded her: "If you don't behave, you'll grow up to marry a *ddong jang-gun*!" *Ddong jang-gun* means Shit General, a man who earns his living emptying septic tanks, a pair of wooden buckets suspended from a pole balanced along his shoulders. They have green trucks now with suction hoses, except in the trickier parts of Pusan, where the *ddong jang-gun* still plies his trade, buckets suspended, dreaming of little Korean girls who must someday grow up.

IV

People here are still unhappy in the memory of the Greater East Asia Co-Prosperity Sphere. During World War II, Korean women were conscripted to serve as "companions" to Japanese soldiers in the field. Hirofumi Ichigawa, fresh from a sweet lay, blew the nuts off Sgt. Mike Corcoran of Billings, Montana, a quiet heterosexual town. On August 6,

1945, at 8:16 AM in Hiroshima, Ichigawa's wife's clitoris disintegrated. United. In a Heaven. We believe.

V

Yes, I visited Ground Zero in Nagasaki. A disappointment. Flowers in bloom, a thick-leaved pungent green. Manicured. A lizard skittered by. One head. Four legs. One tail. Standard. Right out of the manual. A narrow tower of mangled steel. One thinks: WHUMPF! KA-WHAM! But still. The sky a still, placid blue. And then a speck. A black speck.

VI

The Buddha bade farewell to the rats last, it is said, before ascending. At last! they cried, scrambling for the last few crumbs that had lain pressed under the Great One's thighs.

THE GENTLE MONK: A FIRE SERMON

The sky now a low, granular, crematory gray. Up a narrow path behind the temple, a young monk, rustic in his splay-footed gait, head shaven beneath a flat, conical woven hat, carries a shallow basket of tender green sprigs, garnishings for a humble, ascetic's vegetarian repast. He has never tasted of meat, nor ever hopes to. Nor of liquor. Though he has heard tales of his brethren in far off Seoul and Pusan, of women, of wine, of dancing, of crimson laughter and quicksilver song. Of plush restaurants and steaming platters of spiced beef and pork and dog. Of dark pacts concluded and sealed in posh hotel rooms during the chill hours before dawn. Of limousined executives and envelopes stuffed with banknotes and ornamented temples erected on choice parcels of land with proud new courtyard tombs housing the bones of a rich donor's parents. Of lonely wives in rut and a luxurious fur coat hiked to mid-thigh and sly, knowing glances and an oily bald monk's dry, eager mouth. Of the flesh. Of the flesh he knows only the intimate prickle of his skin beneath his coarse robe and his baggy trousers knotted at the waist and gathered at the ankles. Of one thing he is certain: that this morning's erection was a temptation and he did not succumb. That purification of desire is the gaze inward upon the flame that dances upon the Void. That, or Nothing.

A TALE OF TWO PENINSULAS

Washing dishes in
the kitchen sink
of our tiny Pusan
Korea apartment
MK overhears
a CNN news report
about a young man
asleep in his bed
disappearing into
a Florida sinkhole.
She pulls the plug
under the dishwater
and watches it swirl
down the drain. Only
for a moment, for
only the briefest of
moments does she
see me lying on
the sofa and caught
in the maelstrom
reach up and beg
for my life.

IN A STATION OF THE METRO

During the suicide season
the city hires a raft of retirees
to don bright orange vests and
patrol the subway platforms
until the new sliding glass doors
are installed. Who is the more
desperate, one wonders—Metro
Central to avoid the needless
delays a leaper precipitates,
these old geezers in their
eagerness to prove they still
have something on the ball,
or me with my brittle heart
and broken brain—as the train
arrives precisely on time? Was
I the only soul in the crowd
who felt the tug, the nudge
to the ledge, the urge to take
the plunge and what kept me
from jumping? Who knows?
And Nothing, really, I tell
myself, ignoring the horror
I just might soil my shorts.

HAIBUN EPILOGUE

I was reading Brautigan again after so many years. He had not aged well. I looked for the small ruptures that had opened up pathways to momentary insight and joy in my Hippie Youth. Here or there, almost yes. But mostly, almost always no. Whither, I had to ask myself, the magic of those sentences? The laconic spareness of Hemingway and antic mordancy of Twain. Dead on the page. You had to look away. We called him up once long distance – his phone number was printed on the back cover of our early edition – and caught him in a transparent and pointless lie. We forgave him then. He was our hero. But this let down. He drank, or so we heard, to keep his demons at bay. Or perhaps the numbness. Flip sides of the same coin.

She asked me woozily when was I going to turn in. I took off my glasses and rubbed my temples for long minutes, an hour. What would Trout Fishing in America say tonight? Do? I turned a flat page. Nada. I stood up from my chair. My back creaked. The aging, failed poet. The original promise and the blind spots. An occasional flare brightening a narrow auditorium. Followed by the fizzled squibs and clogged apercus. The silent decade. The bouts of sanctimony and envy. Then another equally arid. A stunted comeback and ultimate exile among these alien folk. The rickety haibun sequence and *What happened* of that last rejection letter. The sleeplessness and local hooch. The Booming Voice of Wit and Candor at bottom a cowed and silenced bore.

> Rumble and thunder
> from behind our bedroom door:
> my drunken wife snores

DOWN LETTER HOME TO A POET FRIEND

for Chuck Naccarato

's been too long since I last clapped
my hands and sang at your eye
with all the pieces of your face
in my mind. Sorry. Forgive me.
The days grow short, are money.

Funny.
      I have nothing to say.
I knock out a poem now and again.
You're in them, somewhere. Hell.
Hairs clog the drain. My shit runs
straight out to sea like everyone's
else.

    I smoke and talk and wheeze.
& milk silent at the Bitch of Paradise.
The nights get longer. Write. Please
just don't ever do unto yourself what
I done unto me. Jeez. I can't say
that. I'm happy here. I can leave.

AN ANGEL OF ENGLISH

An Angel of English flooded my room this morning
with sweetness & light & a disturbing request:
She wanted to know what we Earth Huggers
down here make of the state of our Native Tongue
at this late date in the decline of just about everything.

Angel, I said, do you mean you want to find out
if people are happy with their vernacular
if they feel it's still providing them with sufficient
  creative opportunities to express themselves
if there are any peculiar words they would rather
  not have around any longer
if the spelling is still too tough
if they fear vulgarity is on the overall gross increase
if there are enough euphemisms & other circumlocutions
  available for them to negotiate their way through
  the many tricky thickets of potentially embarrassing
  social encounters
if lies are on the rise & what they might be able to do
  about it
if people worry they are telling the ugly truth without
  realizing it too often these days
if they still believe, for instance, in crap like Freudian Slips
if the vocabulary of daily commerce is holding steady
  or diminishing or becoming just too damn unwieldy
if the Language of Love is still as hyperbolic & insipid
  as it has always been – that kind of thing?

Yep, She said, you get my drift. Now tell me—

O Angel, I besought, don't task me to come up with any more
such hard questions about our devilish & beloved English.
I'm just an expat scribbler with too much beer on his morning
breath & too many years away from his native shores.
These days I just go on & on & nobody here or
anywhere else gives a pig's whistle about the words

I use to map the dominion of heartache, Angel,
across the domain of our mundane chance enchantments
with mere flesh. I'm nothing but a crumb bum poet
& you know it & I know it & we all know it.

Crumb Bum, She ejaculated in my ear (yes, Angels do that too).
I haven't heard that one since 1955. Old Man, you made my day.
Now let me make yours. And with that—POOF—she vanished
& this poem was finished & my day was made.

RECOGNITION

You know you're
at home
finally
in a foreign land
among an alien
folk
on the street
in the market
at a bus
stop when
from the face
of a stranger—
strutting young
blade or dolled
up *agashi*
besotted office
drone stumbling
homeward
crinkled sidewalk
auntie peddling
mushrooms
and yams—
the familiar eyes
of an old
friend decades
dead
a perished father
a lover long
gone over to
the Other Side
stare back

B'S CHOREA
A Poet's Journal

Have you ever seen a genius stuffed and mounted?
  Yi Sang, "Wings" (1936)

The typical Korean body, like the Eskimo's, is eminently designed for the harsh, brutal winters. The short arms and legs and elongated torsos present less skin surface to the frigid air—less heat is dissipated off. Breath does not so readily freeze on the chin and upper lip of the scantily bewhiskered man. Korean claims of descent from a primeval She-bear can be discounted.

The typical Korean skull can have decidedly Amerindian features—living, breathing evidence of the Ice Age land bridge across the Bering Strait: high, rounded cheekbones molded into a wise, benignant passivity. Something of an amateur phrenologist, I can sometimes see the skull beneath the skin. Such a skull as In-ja's would stand out in a boneheap. The Capuchins would give her a place of honor in one of their nightmarish tableaux.

Something absolutely must be said of In-ja's butt. Why? And what? Because its open, inviting cleft suggests a freshly baked pie with just the thinnest of slices removed? That's part of it. Because she is typical of her good sisterhood in this obscure corner of the globe? That cannot be denied. It is difficult to believe that this transcendent feature is constructed of little more than spiced cabbage, rice, noodles and seaweed—plus a scosh of genetic material and a good deal of exercise in the squatting position. When I consider this fact, I despair less of the future of humankind.

"Why you alla time touch me there?"
"I'm curious."
"Jejus Kleist, you alla time curious."
"I have to know certain things before I die."
"You not gonna die."
"I'm going to die before you do, that's for sure. Look how healthy and smooth you are."
"I said don't touch me like that!"

In-ja is lying on her belly with the bedsheet thrown to the side. The early afternoon sunlight streams in through the window. I slip the white envelope end-wise in the crack of her bum. It stands up like the sail of a boat.

"What you doing *now*?"
"I'm mailing a letter."
"You think I'm mailing box? Who you send letter to?"
"To America."
"What it says?"
"It says, 'Sniff me, and you'll never go back to toot.'"
"Who's Toot?"
"A rich people's drug."
"You not rich, that for sure."

I take the envelope out of her breech, give it a whiff, and hand it to her. It smells faintly like day-old boiled squid. She sits up, opens the envelope and shakes out the rejection slip I picked up at the P.O. just that morning. She reads:

To me, the manuscript seemed racist and sexist. In fact, I couldn't really find anything likeable in your poems. Is this what you really think of women? You may find fans for "slap the bitch around" / "look at the weird habits of the gooks" writing—there are always going to be men who find that kind of work appealing. But is that what you really want to say to the world? Wake up, man! Charles Bukowski just barely got away with that kind of shit, but I don't think a new writer can—or should—be able to.

She puts the slip back into the envelope, disgusted.
"Kleist on a clutch. When you gonna get a job?"

The Sleeping Beauties: A Chosun Dynasty Chronicle: As highly prized as she is in certain elegant and worldly courts and circles, a virgin with no thatchy apron of modesty between her smooth thighs is considered an omen of ill-fortune here in The Land of the Morning Calm. In the distant provinces she may even be driven from her village after a bad harvest or a well gone dry. Alone in the forest she removes her smock and her underthings and folds them carefully into a pillow to set beneath her heavy head. She stretches out naked in an umbral glade and passes into a deep sleep. For some occult reason the flesh of such a woman does not wither with time, but stiffens into a marmoreal chill forever on death's threshold, as a damp moss fills those hidden slopes and shadowy crevices of the still body that the noontime sun only fleetingly glances. Huntsmen and woodcutters in their weary homeward tread come upon these marvels even today and fall to their knees in awe and adoration, too reverent of the serene slumber to disturb it with an awakening kiss. Only now and then in the twilight do the nibbling deer emerge from the misty foliage, the stags and does and fawns, with their keen noses and nimble tongues and precise cervine teeth, and their craving for the succulent, the tender, the untouched greens of the forest shade.

The Callipygraphian Buddha: Sitting bare-assed on the thick glass platen of the Xerox machine, he pumps in coins—*yen* from Japan, *won* from Korea, *baht* from Thailand, *rupees* from Nepal, *kyat* from Burma, slugs from the practical jokers among his world-wide adherents. Time is short, his mailing list long. Expect your Beatific Smile soon, suitable for framing.

I wake up in the dark—I don't know why. I feel for In-ja in my usual fashion—rolling over and expecting first contact with her bottom. She sleeps like that—fetally—legs drawn up, her pointy bum provocative and available. But it is not there. She is not there. It is only then that I hear it: a kind of strangled moan—a choked weeping. One corner of the room is very dark, and there is some movement, or else the sound is giving movement to the dark that is emitting it.

"In-ja?"

No answer.

"In-ja, turn on the light."

"No-o-o."

"What's wrong?"

There is a funny odor in the air—of snuffed candle wick. She sometimes uses our Love Candle to find her way in the dark if she comes home from work after I have turned in. It has been freshly extinguished.

"Did you just come in?"

"You."

"Me what, baby?"

"*Kee-sheen. Kee-sheen.*"

I know the word: Ghost. And they are very much alive and well in Korea. Few women in the countryside have not seen the Egg Ghost, who makes his rounds of the outhouses in the small farming communities on frosty evenings. Eyeless, noseless, mouthless, he puts in his grand appearance just as the woman has pulled down her drawers and commenced her subterranean rumblings. Often a wife will drag her husband outside to the crapper to stand behind the door and talk to her while she performs. But the Egg Ghost is something of a comical figure. The others are not.

"In-ja, come to bed."

"You. *Kee-shee.*"

"In-ja, what are you talking about?"

"You eyes."

And then I know, I understand. Since childhood, I sometimes fall asleep with my eyes open. And so I don't try to stop her when she stuffs a few clean underthings into her handbag and leaves to spend the night with one of her Russian stripper friends in a room above a Texas Street bar.

To describe a woman leaving a man, the Korean inmates used the phrase "She put her rubber slippers on backward" – meaning the woman was walking away from the house, not toward it as in happier times. (Cullen Thomas, *Brother One Cell: An American Coming of Age in South Korea's Prisons*, 2007.)

The Mongolian Blue Spot is a purplish blotch located just north of the rump on some newborn Korean babes, the color of new wine seeping along capillaries. (Even mixed-bloods may exhibit this genetic anomaly: Western men married to Korean women gaze in horror at this blemish on their newly born and grimly contemplate malpractice suits until they are made to understand it's all in the nature of things.) The Spot disappears gradually and is fully gone by the time the child is weaned from the tit. Rarely does a person retain it until adulthood—as Mi-ja has. Hers is symmetrical and suggestive, like a Rorschach inkblot. I see bat's wings, mitosis, another woman's bush, Siamese-twin trilobites joined at the lips—the usual stuff. I rigged up a series of mirrors so Mi-ja could give me her readings. She sees Wallis' *The Death of Chatterton*, Mike Tyson nibbling on Evander Holyfield's ear, banquet tables upended by sword and muscled arm and mossy stone walls spattered with blood, my face hauled before a tribunal of ghosts—the usual stuff, for her. She doesn't go by the rules, I know, and remains adamant and unrepentant when I tell her she is wrong.

Glimpsed: In the shadows, a braceleted whore walks her hand and long nails up and down the Buddha's tattooed forearm, like a belled and hooded hawk.

In Korea it is *um-yang* rather than the Sinitic *yin-yang*. In pronunciation, the *um* lies somewhere between the *m-m-mm* in the sense of delicious and the *um* that precedes a hazarded guess. Mi-ja has pointed out to me that in order to make this sound properly I must place her taut nipple between my lips and express satisfaction. Some related words:

um: the negative, the passive, secrecy, darkness
um-aek: sperm, semen
um-ak: music
um-ak-ga: a musician
um-boo: mons Veneris
um-chee: tone-deafness; lack of musical ability
um-chook: atrophy of the penis
um-dam: obscene conversation; bawdy talk; lewd stories
um-dok: taking poison
um-duk: a secret act of charity
um-gi: chilliness, dreariness
um-gong: hidden merits
um-guk: the negative pole
um-gyeh: the world of the dead; the shadowy kingdom; the realm of the shades; the nether world
um-gyung: the penis
um-hae: stab in the back
um-haek: the clitoris
um-hum: sneaky, wily, cunning
um-hyoong: wickedness, treacherousness
um-jee-ga yang-jee-dwenda: After the rain comes fair weather.
um-jung sa-ram: a black-hearted man
um-jung-kee: negative electricity
um-mae: a cow's moo
um-mee: lasciviousness, obscenity
um-mo: pubic hair
um-mo-ga: a schemer, a machinater, a mischief maker
um-mo-ja: a plotter, a conspirator, an intriguer

um-mool: a lewd fellow, a licentious person
um-moon: the vulva
um-nang: the scrotum
um-nyo: a lewd woman, an unchaste woman, a woman of loose morals
um-oo: a dreary rain
um-ool: dismal, melancholy
um-ran: lewdness, lechery, lasciviousness
um-ryuk: the lunar calendar
um-san: cloudy and gloomy
um-so: an erotic book, a foul book, obscene literature, pornography
um-soon: the labia
um-sup: shady and damp
um-taek: a grave
um-tam: a taste for lewdness; a hunger for lechery
um-tong-ha-da: to experience sex for the first time
um-tuk: wicked, villainous, knavish
um-ui: impotence
um-wha: a crypt
um-yak: a secret promise or agreement
um-yang: the cosmic dual forces; the male and female principles; the positive and negative; the sun and the moon; shade and light
um-yang-ga: a fortune teller, a diviner, an augur

Mi-ja has been having bad dreams lately, *gae goom* or "dog dreams." Such dreams are said by Koreans to have no meaningful content, as a dog wakes from startled sleep, looks stupidly around, and drops his head back down between his paws again. I suspect she feels guilty about something, and I suppose I know what. She is a bright young woman with an attractive academic career in her future. I sent her a poem about a month ago with the line: *In black sleep our jaws work unknown tongues.* I didn't mean anything by it—I only liked the way it sounded at the time. She wrote back in a letter I got yesterday: *I finished my second portion of drinking Oriental Medication, called Han-Yak. Mom suggested me that I go to see the doctor and get the medication more. I dislike the taste. But I can't help drinking it. Strange sound is resonating into my ear and the wall in my room is moving around. When I'm in the bed, I see hundreds of sharp pins are pouring down upon my face. And also in my dreams I'm dipping my hands into the big loaf of blood. It's moving and strangling my hands and arms and breasts and the whole body. I wake up out of my bed, screaming and sometimes crying. My body and hair are all wet with sweat. Every morning I have to change my underwear. And also in my half dreaming and half waking condition, I grit my teeth so strongly that I can see all the teeth are about to fall out and rotten. I start pulling out those one by one, seeing all the ugly parasites in here, tooth moving and coming out of its hole. My lips are becoming blastered (I'm not sure whether the word is right) and my complexions are getting worse.* Of course I know she has another lover. (Which is why I will soon let myself be taken up by little Un-joo.) Mi-ja betrays me and then complains of the terrors of her oneiric life. Strangely, knowing this appeals to my vanity—as having two lovers no doubt appeals to hers. So we shuttle back and forth our cryptic, encoded messages, getting nowhere. An apt joke on me—and apparently one with no punch line.

The Buddha Trick or Treating: Glowing eyes, a serrated smile—like a jackal lantern.

One description of the human brain requires that you picture a grotesque and deformed homunculus suspended by its heels from the dome of your skull. Like one of those weird demographic maps of the world that show burgeoning, overpopulated South Korea as huge and the vast empty tracts of Mongolia as miniscule, so the limbs and appendages and special zones of the "little man" bulge and swell or shrink according to the concentration of nerve tissue in the corresponding areas of the host body. Enormous are the hands and feet, the fingertips swollen and bulbous like those of a tree frog. The genitals massive beyond anything conjurable by even the most obsessed and demonic imagination. Nipples—even the male's—as big as dinner plates. The anus like the mouth of a volcano. The head tiny and flat-topped, except for the lips, which are broad and thick as the monstrous black tires on one of those saurian earth-movers that are forever rearranging the face of the planet. And the distended tongue: Melvillian, tragic, farcical, impossible to contemplate, a sideshow freak, crashing through the bushes at night, alien, feared, and rooted in the insensate heart.

In the past, Korean men who married women who were sisters referred to themselves as *Goo-mung Dong-suh*, or Same Hole Brothers-in-Law. Sisters, it seems, were but extensions of one fleshly entity, identical ripe melons on a single familial vine. Times change, however, and with them morals and the meanings of popular figures of speech. Today, men are Same Hole Brothers-in-Law when they happen to be sleeping with the same woman, like a pair of golfers (or even a threesome or a foursome) on the same pristine, dewy green stroking their tensed and dimpled balls toward a shared cup.

    The Korean word for female breast is *yoo-bahng*, literally "milk room." One imagines a mosque-like dome filled with sterilized stainless steel canisters. One imagines a closed cell filling slowly with the precious white liquid until the penitent's nose bangs against the ceiling and there is no more air. One imagines a woman built like a house. One imagines walking down long darkened doorless corridors, lost. One imagines meeting her other lost lover on a staircase. One imagines asking directions, trusting. One imagines giving directions, and lying. One has known from birth that there are two breasts, two "milk rooms," and that a single pair of lips cannot occupy both of them at the same time. One has known from birth that one must go from one nipple to the other, checking, endlessly.

    Mi-ja!

Saith The Edgar Allan Buddha: You either live on the edge—
or in the Pit. (Soused on ardent fluids once again)

Un-joo comes over on a lazy Sunday to steam me some fresh clams American style. She has clipped a recipe from the local English-language newspaper, which occasionally carries kitchen hints for Korean wives and "friends" of Western men. Sitting on the bedroom floor revising some lies I have written, I hear her at the top of her lungs:

"YOU GODDAM CLAMS! YOU ARE GOOD FOR NOTHING! I WORK MY FINGER TO A BONE AND YOU COME HOME STINKY OF SOJU AND YOUR PANTS IS FILTHY! OTHER CLAMS THEY DON'T STAY OUT ALL NIGHT IN A POJANG-MACHA OR A ROOM SALON SKEEZING A TIT OF A BUSINESS GIRL! WIPE A SMILE OFF YOUR FACES! AND DON'T YOU STICK A LONG SKINNY TONGUE AT ME! SURE— YOU DON'T WANNA TALK NOW! MAYBE I GONNA HAVE TO SHOW YOU WHO'S A BOSS HERE!"

I get up off the floor and walk into the kitchen. Un-joo is red-faced, her tiny body trembling.

"What's going on, darling?"

"I got to scold a clams in boiling water."

"What are you talking about?"

"Cause of a recipe say so."

"Let me see that."

She hands me the clipping. Suspicious, I give it a quick read.

"Baby, this is a misprint. The proofreader fucked up again. It should say *Clean the clams and scald them in boiling water*. Not *scold* them."

"Oh."

"Why in the hell would you scold a clam?"

"I DON'T KNOW," she cries from behind a veil of tears. "I NEVER BEEN TO ENGLISH AMERICA! I DON'T KNOW!"

And I couldn't really blame her. As an American, I don't understand the nuances of the sport of soccer. Just a week ago a misprint on the Sports Page gave me momentary pause as it chalked a rather improbable maneuver across the blackboard of my imagination: "Pletikosa made an impressive debut in last week's match, shitting out Montenegro's dangerous striker, Vujovic."

Ouch! And on a holy Sunday!

The Buddha as Gagman: If you say something amusing, and nobody laughs, is it funny or not? Thus pondered the Great One on his solitary seat in a glade, bowing occasionally to the din of a single hand clapping.

Dear B,

Hi, I don't know how to begin with. First of all, I say I will not see you again. I have been dating out with a man for a couple of years. I decided to get married with that guy. The reason I have been meeting with you is that 1) early this year I needed a physical partner desperately. I mean I wanted to do it. But the guy didn't accept my suggestion of having it. So I looked around and you were there. Don't be angry. I didn't use you. I didn't love that guy. We were just friends. But things have been changed. I love the man. I want to marry him. 2) as you're the first man to win me, I felt a sort of affection. So I thought I had to come to you to get together even once a month.

      He found out the relationship between you and me. Nowadays I have been irritable to think of handling my dilema. He got suspicion of me. Last Saturday when we had dinner together, he went to his car where my bag which has your letter and poem was. I told him the story. Feeling shame about our first meeting when you plucked me, I told him we were only a Plutonic relationship. He believed me I think. "And also the last time of our meeting was last weekend of August," I said to him. I missed my period. Anyhow that's all. Would it be all right if I asked you a favor? Send my blacken white pictures (including film), please. Thanks.

Take care!!
Mi-ja

P.S. He is a nice person. I don't think you have to worry about his retaliation about us. He's a man of integrity and virtue. He will not do what you may worry.

As a Texas Street whore once put it to the Buddha: Come on. I give you good time. All night—I no care about long time. You watch a clock, it never gonna boil.

Um-chee is a fascinating expression in Korean. It can mean either 1) Vagina Dentata (*um*=female netherness; *chee*=tooth) or 2) Tone Deaf (*um* from *um-ak*, music; *chee* from *chee-gwa*, dentist: A person with a "tin ear" is said to have a mother who is a piano tuner and a father who is a dentist—that is, a cross between the two.) I am a victim of the latter condition and jig to a very different tune from those around me. I have met only one woman here who is *um-chee* in the former sense. She had only uppers, the dentition fused as in some lower animals or a boxer's white mouthpiece. She allowed me to run my finger along her edge. It was smooth, like the spine of a plastic pocket comb, and moist. We did not engage in sexual congress, as she was afraid she might hurt me. (She has asked me not to reveal her identity, though by now you know her name—and I've loved her in her more normal incarnations.) The experience is still quite vivid in my memory. Even hours after waking up, I remained convinced the episode was genuine.

When Un-joo was a child, she and her mother were dirt poor. Whenever her mother left to seek work in a far-off village—carrying faggots down out of the hills to sell as kindling to strangers—Un-joo was shuttled from poor household to poor household in her village as a sort of adjunct step-child. And so it was her lot to be left sucking hind tit, so to speak. In one home there was a shortage of rice bowls and Un-joo had to eat out of a tin dog's dish. Some eighteen years later, she remembers every tiny nick and scratch on the thing. She recalls even the subtle shadings of its worn patina. She can still taste the metallic flavor it lent to her meager share of rice. ("Barley," she corrects me. "In those days we had only barley to eat, though we called it *bop*, rice, wishfully.") She remembers it all with impressive exactitude—with a curious mixture of shame and good humor now. I am many years her senior. She visits me often these days, bringing gifts of fruit and Marlboros. She has a good job at the local branch of Philips Consumer Lifestyle and enjoys buying things for people, especially food. When I sit and drink beer at my kitchen table, she settles at my feet and I stroke her long hair. If she had a tail, I suspect she would wag it. And, in her own special way, she does.

The magpie plays an important role in Korean folk medicine. Magpie tongues are eaten to heal bloody boils, and post-partum mothers crave magpie meat.

These rather harmless remedies are joined by more adventurous and hair-raising ones. When a young girl dies of smallpox, the corpse is wrapped in straw and hung from a solitary tree. As it decomposes, the drippings are collected and used as a cure-all. (Dr. Norbert Weber, O.S.B., *Im Lande der Morgenstille*, 1923.)

The Buddha to the Dark Tower Came: A crenellated smile, like an orthodontist's bastard child.

Un-joo has always sensed a curious link between food and education. As a penniless and famished pre-schooler loitering anonymously among groups of older kids, she overheard tales of bread and milk and the singing of happy songs taking place at the village school. To her, such a place had to be akin to Paradise—an outpost on the road to Heavenly Grace and a Full Belly. On mornings when her mother's "rice" pot contained only the burnt crust of the previous evening's meager meal, she would stand outside the dilapidated schoolhouse like a tiny statue—almost a lawn ornament—listening to the lucky students inside repeating in unison their rote lessons. To her "5 times 7 equals 35" had to be a magical incantation filling a warm tumbler of milk from the bottom up, as if fed from a mysterious underground spring. To her "Paris is on the Seine River" was the secret formula for dividing a sweet cake into a thousand pieces, each the size of the original Mother Loaf.

Occasionally reduced to prowling hungrily for handouts door to door, Un-joo once popped in on a family who quickly hid the ears of sweet corn they had only just passed around the table. She still recalls the bright yellow cylinders disappearing as of their volition, and the unique and ineffable solitariness of an unwanted intruder at a stingy family's repast. A few years later, after her mother had finally tucked away enough spare change to pay her entrance fee, Un-joo stood at the edge of the playground on her first day of school. The daughter of the Ears of Sweet Corn Family pranced gaily up to her and cried "Hello!" in innocent and girlish glee. Un-joo froze, the perfect rote memory of hunger seizing her in the way calculations can suddenly immobilize even the most fluid of minds, and then burst into a howl of wild laughter that sounded like arithmetic problems and foreign capitals and the exact dates of important feast days around the globe.

The Buddha at Whack-a-Mole: Quietly the North Koreans have been digging tunnels under the DMZ, the Demilitarized Zone. In the readers of South Korean first graders, the North Koreans are snouty rats in army fatigues, forever burrowing away with red stars on their caps. The South Koreans are depicted as friendly farm animals: a buck-toothed and mild-tempered horse in bib overalls, a bearded and grandfatherly he-goat, a chubby and pink Petunia Pig full of good cheer and neighborly concern. In a surprise attack, the North Korean rats pour out of their underground hideouts. The South Korean farm animals, alerted by a plucky barnyard chanticleer, fend off the invasion with pitchforks and beat the intruders back into their holes with large wooden spoons. A grand celebration follows, a moo-cow and her swollen udder swaying under a harvest moon.

CHOREA (from the Greek *khoreia*, "dance," and pronounced *KOREA*): a nervous disorder (as of man or dogs) marked by spasmodic movements of the limbs and facial muscles and by incoordination.

One of the most impressive features of a Korean woman's torso is the long vertical muscle holding her guts in, the *rectus abdominis*. Well-developed below the navel, it is what gives her body that faintly marsupial look. Korean women, however, will tell you they have two stomachs: the *weet bae* (upper stomach) and the *ddong bae* (shit stomach). And if you ever watched tiny Un-joo spoon down her second bowl of rice after a full meal of grilled seasoned ribs, steamed ark shell clams, stir-fried anchovies with peppers, jellied mung-bean puree, garland chrysanthemum salad, lettuce leaves and shredded leeks in hot pepper sauce, yams in syrup, soy-sauce glazed lotus root, and half a bottle of Mu-hak ("Dancing Crane") soju, you just might begin to believe it.

I Sing the Body Eclectic: The Western Look at a few hundred bucks a peeper. The tv commercials are full of beauties with rounded, doll-like eyes. The operation, in which a smidgen of fatty tissue is removed from behind the eyelid, is quick and painless, recovery only slightly uncomfortable. Nose bridges can be raised to lend a sense of depth to the setting of these jewels so recently unearthed. Dimples as simple as pumping a couple of BBs into a lump of dough.

In Korea a magpie's *gack gack gack* near your front door is said to be a harbinger of good fortune for you and your household, often heralding the arrival of an old friend. This morning on tv I caught an old Heckle and Jeckle cartoon dubbed in Korea. The two antic magpies spent the better part of the episode dashing up and down a set of department store escalators, pausing when they collided with each other on the escalator landings to exchange their trademark wisecracks before resuming flight from an exasperated dog-faced bully in a policeman's uniform. I laughed. It was like running into a couple of old childhood playmates who suddenly fall into a long forgotten madcap schoolyard routine—in Korean.

  Then in the afternoon In-ja phones, a bolt out of the blue, after so many months, and we meet in a downtown café. She's down from Seoul to minister to an ailing mother. We stroll through Jagalchi fishmarket along the docks, admiring the corvina and cutlass fish and the red snappers laid in even rows in the stalls, their glassy dead walleyes gazing up at a Nothing In Particular world. In-ja asks me if I still fall asleep with my eyes open sometimes. We laugh. I ask her if she has yet to sprout a single hair on her immaculate and hairless Venereal eminence, sleek as a cue ball. We laugh and I tell her about Rogaine and its miracle ingredient. She listens with feigned interest as the bouquet of the fishmarket engulfs us, and suddenly it all comes back to me, word for word, that strange footnote that so deepened and thwarted my love of cunnilingus in a more amorous, more innocent age: *Merely in passing will I refer to the peculiar fact that the genital secretion of the female among the higher mammals and in man, the erotically stimulating effect of which, as we have said, may be traceable to infantile reminiscences, possesses a distinctly fishy odor (odor of herring brine), according to the description of all physiologists; this odor of the vagina comes from the same substance (trimethylamine) as the decomposition of fish gives rise to.*

Later, in the subway, we say goodbye without having made love, marooned as we are on dry land, on islands steadily drifting apart.

The wild sheaf of hair wrapped in gray monk's robes and slumped in a dark corner of a back alley: The Buddha, hooked on minoxidil.

My, what a long tail you have say Korean mothers to children who dash into the house without closing the door after themselves. In America, of course, it is: *Hey, were you born in a barn or what?*

I said this to Un-joo the afternoon she burst into my apartment to announce that a neighbor woman was having at her jobless husband, like Cora running down Mr. Dithers with a rolling-pin clenched in her fist in the old Dagwood comics.

"Yes," she said, "I was. Between two cows, in fact."

The outhouse at her grandmother's, it turned out, had been attached to an open, doorless structure that served as a shelter for the few farm animals the old woman had been able to afford to keep. Un-joo's mother, unwedded and big with child, had gone to answer Nature's call one evening. Squatting in the frosty darkness, she glimpsed something shadowy and menacing and felt her water break. She managed to crawl only as far as the middle of the "barn" when little Un-joo came clawing her screaming, bloody entrance into the world. She was a tiny, tough baby, more animal than human, a fighter, so undersized that her mother could hold her easily in the palm of her hand. Twice during the ensuing months—as it became increasingly evident that the Japanese mariner who was the baby's natural father was not going to show up—Un-joo's mother took her little bundle of illicit love and laid it down on the exact spot between the brace of tired, old beeves where the whole miserable business of her motherhood had begun in the first place. She hoped that Fate would guide one of the beasts' ponderous, blind hooves right smack down on the soft, spongy skull of the howling bag of infant guts. But Fate, or the cows, lacked sufficient interest in human affairs, and Un-joo survived those two long identical winter nights in her windy, ramshackle incubator of death, the cows' murderous feet thudding down in some random untraceable choreography that did not include a baby's head. Sometime later, her mother gave it one more shot and dumped Un-joo off on a mountainside, the favored place of abandonment for unwanted infants and the unbearable, inconsolably aged. But the mountainside was too near the house and Un-joo's lungs too strong. The grandmother heard her squalls and brought her back into the warm indoors. This was the last straw—Un-joo's mother gave up and accepted her lot.

Eleven years later, on a visit to her grandmother's isolated farmhouse to wheedle a little money for schoolbooks and pencils, Un-joo listened to the addled old woman relate the sorry details of Un-joo's birth and her three brushes with the Hereafter. Horrified, Un-joo dashed down to the village where she now lived and burst in on her mother, who was busy shoveling a few pieces of kindling under a cooking pot.

"What a long tail you have, Un-joo," her mother said.

Un-joo stopped in mid-wail, shut the door behind her, and proceeded to let fly so furious a cascade of accusations and indignation that immediately her mother knew the jig was up. Villagers crowded around the door and single window of the cramped one-room house to savor the wrath of a bastard girl-child born in a barn and thrice nearly murdered by her own mother. Only by nightfall had Un-joo exhausted her rage and the two females fell into one another's arms, weeping, forgiven and forgiving, abandoned and abandoned. In small groups the villagers returned to their homes, fattened on the misery of others and a renewed appreciation of their own superior moral worth.

"What a long tale you have, Un-joo," I said.

She blinked, sitting at my feet, and glanced at the door of the apartment.

"It's closed," she said. "I closed it because of you asked me if I was borned in a barn."

"So you did," I said. "Good girl."

La Buddha Gioconda: An undulate smile, like a *kris*.

"But I don't want to marry him!"

It was Un-joo – again. This had been going on for three days now, the phone calls.

"Then don't."

"But I said I would meet him this afternoon. What can I tell him?"

"That you don't love him."

"But he doesn't care! He says that will change!"

I said nothing – as I had said nothing at this point in the conversation yesterday and the night before that. I pitied her the brutality of having to make choices, and I envied her the illusion that there really were choices to be made. This "he" was an American Air Force medical officer – a shrink, in fact. Fed up with the intransigence of American women, he wanted "Oriental". On the beach outside Pusan he had stumbled upon sweet little Un-joo and knew what he had. I had to hand him that. They had been together for six weeks, going no further than holding hands. Then he left Korea for a year, calling her from the States weekly, tenaciously. He offered a new Toyota and a college education. Her younger sister, whom she was putting through high school, could join the household. Now he was back – for a week.

"Well, you will change," I said.

"But I don't love him. Can't you help me?"

"It's not my decision. It's yours."

"But I can't."

"Then marry him," I said.

I hung up and unplugged the phone from the wall, feeling the old grievance. Against American money and its cocksureness about love. Against Asian female submissiveness and docility. Against the same old story.

In the freezer compartment of my second-hand Samsung refrigerator, I keep a small soapstone Buddha, seated in the lotus position, a sort of household mountain-top shrine. When I open the door, a light comes on behind his head, just like in the old paintings. When I close the door, the light, presumably, goes out and the Buddha is plunged into frosty darkness. Late at night the compressor clicks on and the apartment is pervaded by a low, even hum. Sometimes I start from sleep in the wee hours with a strange taste in my mouth, like burnt electricity.

You will live to hate its guts if you live there. Perhaps there is no luck in a Peninsula. Ernest Hemingway (One of 47 failed draft attempts to end *A Farewell to Arms*)

MUSING MISS KIM

A Phantasmagoria

During the first year of King Moonmoo's reign (AD 661) the body of a huge woman came floating on the sea south of Sabi-su. Her body was seventy-three feet long, her feet six feet long, and her mount of Venus three feet long.

The Samguk Yusa Book 2 Wonder II

ART

My poems come back to me in the mail from the States with the same complaint every single time: "The guy says we don't fucking work for him." So I take them into the bathroom and scour their mouths with a censoring agent. Of course, it was the same way when I was young and rough-edged and raffish. You go to an interview half-stoned and William Randolph Hearst takes you aside and asks what you would do if Viet Nam erupted right in the middle of your paper route. The one of my poems who is pure Amerasian should have had no problem with a challenge like this, so I sent him off to the Culture Wars, but the point he had to make came back urinated on and scraped off the page, an ugly matrix of cicatrices. Worse, I hadn't xeroxed him beforehand and can't recall what that part of him used to look like. Luckily he had signed an organ donor card and I am still able to use pieces of him I find lying around here. But the rest of him is gone: I can sit here and stare at that stained and shredded trooper till I'm blue in the face and hear nothing but the whimpering of words failing me, like a mother unzipping a body bag to sort out her son. This is grief until I remind myself that I'm alive in Pusan, South Korea. Look at your map – the very tip of the coccyx (Greek *kokkyx*: cuckoo) of Asia! One more step backwards and you're in the drink! I'm here – a cornered dog – and writing! To those of you who are listening.

DOMESTICITY

One night last month when Miss Kim and I got back home from seeing the new American spy-thriller *The Bastard File*, we heard the tell-tale skittering as soon as the tumblers in the lock clicked over. I pushed open the door and Miss Kim made a dash for her broom. I found where the filthy critter had bundled stray strands of Miss Kim's hair in a neat conical shock, like a tiny sheaf of black straw in a harvested field, a sort of gauntlet thrown down. Miss Kim broomed under the sink, a logical refuge, but came up empty. I had warned her a thousand times not to bring a rat-tail comb into the apartment, that they sometimes go feral if you leave them alone for just one evening, and now we had a Situation on our hands. We rounded up all the grooming aids that we thought might join the renegade if rumors began to spread that it was at-large and basking in liberty like Emiliano Zapata's white stallion in the mountains outside Oaxaca: all of Miss Kim's various combs and wooden-handled brushes (including the boar's bristle neither of us had ever really trusted), my nail clippers, her emery boards, her wryneck toothbrush and my electric one (which got the idea it was a vibrator one morning in the bathroom and made a lunge for Miss Kim's crotch while still clutched in my right hand), the nit-comb my mother gave me to use on my mustache, the weird pair of mechanical lips with which Miss Kim curls her eyelashes, everything we could think of that might turn on a master or mistress in the wee hours of revolutionary fervor. I boxed them all up in cardboard and taped them in. Only then could we retire in peace of mind, though we knew we'd be doing this every night till we cornered the rat-tail and scotched him into silence for good. Toward dawn I woke up bathed in a cool, sticky liqueur of fear. "What is it, yobo?" said Miss Kim. *Yobo* is marital Korean for honey, sweetheart, darling, dear, dear-heart, snookums, and baby doll all rolled up into one affectionate ball, though none of them specifically. "The broom!" I croaked. "We forgot to lock up the broom!" "Oh, I can't believe of *that*. Broom he must be loyal as a old horwoarse." (She meant warhorse.) But she followed me into the kitchen and there we beheld a mis-en-scene that would have enticed tears out of even the most cynical of clogged ducts. On the linoleum lay Miss Kim's trusty broom, its faithful worn bristles chewed and cracked and splintered, its smooth shaft now nicked and gouged and scraped. Around it was scattered what was left of the rat-tail, its spine shattered in three places and half its teeth knocked out. "I told you of so," said Miss Kim. After we had tossed it all in the trash and she had gone back to sleep, I gave the sealed cardboard box a shake like a Christmas present and heard the electric toothbrush inside switch on like an angry rechargeable infant roused from innocent slumber: *Wehehehehe!*

TECHNIQUE

For me the hardest thing about scripting up one of these episodes is having to move people around, like a City Transit Authority. Sometimes I even have to lift Miss Kim's hand to her lips so she can take a drag on a cigarette or blow a kiss or stifle a yawn. This is because in general people are lazy, particularly when they are not real. Consequently here at Musing Miss Kim we don't bother to ask people to move at all. If they appear and say something short and to the point like "Where the blazes am I?" we are happy. Then they can de-appear, for all we care. In fact, they don't even have to be able to move their vocal cords, due to our state-of-the-art ventriloquism. Of course, once in a while we audition a character who has ambition and really wants to *move*. We sit her down and tell her that today she's going to play a corpse. Then we lay her out in candlelight and soft music and train our two dozen movie cameras on those areas of her face that are most likely to twitch. The tension is unbearable. Camera jockeys fall off their hydraulic chairs and have fits mimicking epilepsy but more rollicky. Our stockroom is full of remarkable footage, notably for the howls in the background. Once we have a candidate as near Stillness as possible, so still she's having New Age After Death experiences inside her soul, we all crouch down on either side of her ears and shout OKAY HONEY YOU'RE HIRED RISE AND SHINE AND JOIN THE TEAM. The period of bodily awakening that transpires is remarkable for both its brevity and the alacrity of arousal. We see ourselves as guides as well as employers. We have received many letters of appreciation for this method, all of them scribbled in inscrutable dyslexic ink.

ORPHODONTIA

Of a sultry summer afternoon Miss Kim takes me to visit the orphanage where she was deposited just days after her slide past the dentes vaginae and out the exquisite flexible doors of her birth mother. The headmistress is a kindly nun with a face like the front end of a forklift. ("Are those tusks growing out the corners of her mouth?" I whisper to Miss Kim.) The old lady wheezes as she lumbers up the stairs ahead of me to show me where my soulmate once bedded down with forty other "urchints," as she calls them in cacological English, in the girls' dorm. I make a mental note of the electrical cord scraping the floor behind her from beneath the hem of her habit. With one hand she tries to whisk away the smoke rolling out her nose and ears as she points with the other to a space on the floor where on a pallet Miss Kim once curled up in fetal somnolence. "I'm burning up," the goodly Sister says. "It's the heat. When I was a quaint young novice I used to have visions of red-hot shish-ka-bob skewers lancing a purple bubo on my coccyx. I know, I know. All that went out with Santa Teresa. If I'd paid more mind to my Latin, I'd be a Mere Superieure by now. But *No-o-o*. I thought I could become a Saint. And have a mouthful of erections to boot – anagogically speaking, of course." She has a funny way of talking with those tusks sticking out the sides of her face like she's chewing on a couple of stogies. The way old grouches in bowling alleys used to talk in the golden days before malls. "What happens if I plug you in?" I venture. "Oh that. I'd probably turn into the girl of your dreams and drop to my knees and extol your toothsomeness completely out of proportion to your own sense of self-worth right here on the spot. But don't bother. You'd always remember me as the Ganeesha I am now." And just as I am eyeing the electrical outlet on the wall Miss Kim breezes in.

For the first time since we fell in together I take to heart the prominence of the enjambed, staccato dentition behind her lips. And grinding my own grim and squeaky and occasionally falsetto choppers, for the first time in my eternal voyeurhood I begin to ponder how much sinodontic braces run.

CLASS

This morning I woke up convinced that I was Ovid. He was a famous writer and would have been a big fan of mine, style-wise, had he lived to know we've never slept with any of the same women we write about. Since I know almost zilch about the guy and don't look like his schnozz-less busts, I have to improvise. At breakfast I read the fine print on the back of my exile's passport like a cereal box. So many countries I dasn't visit! Then I wonder if they are going to do this to Mars, which like North Korea is always red and angry. And I'd probably get the imperial treatment there, especially if they thought I had a moniker like Publius Ovidius Naso, a.k.a. The Nose. Mars is one of the many who got a piece off of wobbly Venus, like Arthur Miller and Joe DiMaggio and Anchises. I imagine old Ares would like that written up fancy in a literary magazine. Then I pick up the *Aeneid* to check out the lineages and decide I'm not going through that august crate of scrolls again. Too much war and its hell of an aftermath. I once visited Cumae on the arm of a Neapolitan curatrice who bore a striking resemblance to my Miss Kim but all we found left of the Sibylline chthonic mutterances were the gruntings of dwarf pigs rooting around the brush for truffles and other buried delicacies. Fuck divining and research. It's easier to make things up as you weave along. You press your flat snout to the grindstone of the museum and just try to enjoy the tapestry.

CHINOISERIE

Suddenly this summer barefoot on the beach Miss Kim treads on a shard and gets a *bang-koo.* The Korean *bang-koo* means flat-tire in English, though mispronounced *bang-koo-wee* it can also mean fart – an earthy tongue, Miss Kim's. I loosen the lug nuts first, as you're supposed to do, and set the saddle of the jack in her crotch and start pumping till I have her clear of the sand. A crowd of beachurchins gathers around as she teeters up there on her fulcrum and I wrestle with her foot. The damn thing won't come off. I sweat and grunt like the drudge I once was at Thom McAn's, and she moans and coos up there on her perch. They say crippled people come to love the snug fit of the crutch in their armpits. I wonder what would happen if I have to leave her here to get help, but I know in an hour she'd be stripped down to her frame. The beachurchins are already whispering how to prise off her ears. In a tight squeeze culture where anything that sticks out sooner or later gets lopped off, there's always a blackmarket shortage of side-view mirrors. And still the damn foot won't come off. Slowly I realize she's all tensed up – nobody's ever done it to her like this in public before. She feels the eyes of the beachurchins fastened to her body like medicinal leeches on florid swellings. I have breached a cultural taboo. Gently I unjack her and let the air siss out of her good foot fart-wise so at least she's balanced. She wobbles beside me down the strand with pain scribbled across her face like the wail of a mandarin's footbound daughter being signed up for toe-dancing lessons. Sometimes wherever you are whatever you try to be good at doesn't work. "Like floating," laments formerly pneuma-podal Miss Kim, wading ankle-deep in surf she once like swift Camilla so lightly skimmed along.

PEN(W(O))MANSHIP

Onward and Awkward might serve as a fair clinical description of the case of evolutionary heebie-jeebies I have had to endure since the recent capitulation of the slightly sway-backed but nonetheless anatomically correct Miss Kim to certain suggestions I made regarding the human coccyx. Now I don't think I have to tell you that when the early hominoid ape first stood straight up the better to peer into the holes in her mate's skull, a narrowing of the birth canal was forced like closed forceps and gave womankind a copyright on the exclamation "Woe is me." Of course, the editors at Copyright didn't catch the bad grammar – it should read "Woe is I." Or maybe "Woe am I." Nor did they nab T.S. Eliot when he should have said "Let us go then, you and *me*." When I pointed this out at Duke they invited me to mascot their Ivory Tower basketball team, in spite of I'm only five-five and fleshy as plucked pullet and a somatotype closer to that of a dugong. Can't dribble either, though you can learn this by following the instructions of the bouncing ball. When you look at a girl cheerleader leap up and do splits in the air, you are reading a sign that was penned long back in the mistiness of time, when it was harder to see and you really had to jump around to get your message across. It was an attempt, of course, to open up the locks on that canal, to say "Walking upright may have freed my hands to do the laundry, but the missionary position has no real future." I tell all this to my love Miss Kim, who, raised a Confucian, turns it into an ideogram, one curiously resembling the parentheses surrounding the invocative O.

DEREGULATION

Miss Kim has a brand-new broom, a sleek imported job with fiery red bristles I picked up on the black market for a tidy sum. We joke that she could probably make it all the way to Hong Kong on the thing. To "fly to Hong Kong" is Korean slang for a female's reaching orgasm, no mean achievement in a culture which regards moaning and thrashing during sexual congress as an insult to one's ancestors, to say nothing of the neighbors. I'm told The Widow Kwak from across the hall considers me an Ugly American Incarnate when I crank up the volume on Miss Kim and she starts to really flap her arms and rotate her clenched fists like she's ready to take off. I slide her bum around till she's facing straight down the runway and pedaling like crazy, and then, figuratively speaking, I get the hell out of the way. "How was Hong Kong?" I ask her, later, as she hits the ground running. She sighs like a piston sucking in empty air. "Like a Garden of Hedon. Where Sodom and Eve got eated by that Snack." At moments like this I want to break down and laugh. I should never let her get up so high where everything happens in crystal. Sometimes I worry she might never make it back down, though I know from my own annals she could land a Spad on the moon. As she whispers, "Thanks for the new broom."

TRANSPARENCE

By now you have probably guessed that the title on this little exercise is the furthest thing from the truth, though in English. Actually, it is the work of an Invisible Hand, possibly the same one that keeps prodding a stick up Capitalism's ass to keep it awake. My writing desk is littered with invisible nail parings, but I can see them well enough because the dirt on their undersides is just regular dirt. Which is also why Claude Raines was always in the shower. They are okay on tacos – if you like *real* Mexican. I wonder how many tip-toe poems What's Her Face has penned comparing them (not the tacos, sadly) to the moon? Actually, again, the moon is invisible too – all you really see is the dirt on it. The essential unclothed moon-part has never been beheld by the lewd eye. So her trope is apt, if a trifle underblown. The sun is just the opposite – it's so bright you can't see the dirt on it at all, like straight-A students, but this will change as we develop the skills to utilize it as a Cosmic Dumpster. As if the sun were not toxic enough as it is – forcing creatures to grow hair or scales where it's already hot as hell, as on Komodo. Now you're about to ask the question Can An Invisible Hand Get Sunburnt? And the answer is an emphatic Ahem. The sun's beams, which are in fact "pencils of light" – or so they taught us in Physiques for Poets 101 whilst I gnawed the glossy paint off my yellow No. 2 – are the very pencils the Invisible Hand uses to write and then move on. QED

IDENTITY

And also by now you have probably begun to suspect that I have a face that is just run-of-the-mill. Would I could lay those suspicions aside like oars, but the galley of my ordinariness slips forward through tepid seas. Sometimes Miss Kim walks up to strange foreign ordinary seamen on the streets of Pusan and starts chatting with them, thinking they're me. (In the land of the almondine, all round eyes look alike.) Then she gets mad because she decides I'm trying to screw her all the time, satyriasis skulking behind polite conversation. You have to lean back a league just to stroke the old tub of the fixed ego half an inch forward. And the little suction cups that sprout on your blistered palms don't make you feel any better, though it's easier to climb masts. Or grab Miss Kim on the bare behind so's she can't wriggle away. I've thought about locking her up in a brig and hanging myself from a yardarm, but she doesn't care for Billy Buddha sea chanteys. You've got to try to find a way to explain yourself another way. You lift your face out of the common mold and peel off the excess, and stand around waiting for people to tell you what you look like. And it doesn't help when they speak only in clicks and chirps and bos'n's whistles. And the truth is we're not much ready for the truth yet, anyway.

INTEGRATION

Miss Kim is studying to become a real American. I told her that when Americans get together they don't speak textbook English, but in Homophones. This was a cruel lie, but fun. I drill her by firing off a phrase at her and she lobs it back Homophoned. "Baltimore Orioles," I say. "Bald demure aureoles," she replies, and I give her left one a peck. Sometimes I cheat and serve up something quite inconsequential like "The sky god who cares" which on her end comes out "This guy got hookers." I love to look into her eyes during the interval between her utterance of one of these improprieties and that moment when the enormity of it dawns on her. It is like watching the sun come up on a landscape littered with human brainstorms. You want to walk out there and pick one up and hold it to your ear like conch. But the whispering you hear will not be that of the sea. It will be the sound of what goes on between the female half of the human brain and the male half on their Analyst's couch. The female half says it wants to hop in the saddle for the next epoch in the evolution of human consciousness, but the male half says it isn't finished pulverizing the elements yet. Secretly the female half has been busy uncrating large statues of women in armor called Archetypes – which is the mental equivalent of pumping iron – each with a mons-plate as sleek and hard as the gray front end of a bathtub Porsche. Lately the male half has been dozing a lot and sleeps right through the creak of nails being prised out of boards. If Dagwood ever gets up off the sofa and gapes out the window, he's going to notice that the neighborhood has changed. I tell all this to Miss Kim and she looks at me like I just rolled off a porch swing out of a stupor. "Any woman can know already of this. Brain too much think gone a fuck up *Um-*

Yang. Like two buttocks spread apart when guy got a squat. Anal Hissed crouch is middle. And outcome You Know What!"

GILLAGAIN

Perhaps the most erotogenically exciting event a man can experience in life at sea is to steam into a port city known chiefly for its whores. They say Robinson Crusoe constructed a row of brothels out of palm fronds and flotsam futtocks and jetsam jibbooms and waited for the hookers to sprout out of the compost of his memory like mushrooms in a cave. When that didn't happen he sat down on a palm stump and wrote out *Moll Flanders* in a cursive so elegant it slithered right by his self-censor. One night he even arrested his very own person for indeliberate behavior – using his nom-de-surete, Clouseau (Thank you, Miss Kim, for the Asiatic pronunciation cue) – and stood up at his trial and in a self-headlock learned on the stocks read from the text of himself. This made the book the most popular on the island and bathed him in glory. Even the cannibals loved it once he taught them to decipher. Crusoe called Moll his heroine but the savages all labeled her a slut, loitering around the futtock-frond-jibboom stews waiting for her to show up, much as I hang around the kitchen and wait for Miss Kim to pop naked and glistening out of my brain like Athena unarmored can pop out of a hot shower. It's the steaming into port that's exciting, I said, balanced here on the slick fo'c'sle of my fancy like Lem Gulliver on Glumdalclitch's Brobdingnagian mons, a Little Man in a Freudian Boat, remembering Marseilles.

FATE

I digest my thoughts and try to follow them whither they are wont like a frogman of the psychic realm. Most of them go to just keeping my ass out of trouble. Miss Kim gets a big share, these days. These were warped from the beginning anyhow, though I don't tell her that. One thought is about Euclid and won't break down. I think it's still inside the stomach in my brain, rattling around. It's always the truly ossified thoughts that do that. Another thought is useless and completely wrong because it is a conviction that "vertigo" is a color. Too bad you can't push a thought out a 12th story window to teach it a lesson. (Or maybe you can – I've never really tried, being a Thinker.) At about this point in my pursuit my scuba gear goes haywire and I start to get the bends. I try to cry out *Mercedes!* but the words are trapped inside little psychotic bubbles and float gradually away from me like a glass of oxygen-flavored Kool Aid in a drowning dieter's dream. Then I black out and wake up and I'm standing in a sort of Hall of Fame of Thoughts. The busts of famous thoughts are all draped in dust-covers as if they were dead or maybe just on vacation. I take off my flippers and read the instructions on the soles and find that whatever famous thought I choose to unveil will be mine, night and day, until the day or night I die. And I won't even get credit for entertaining it or laving its pensive feet in spermaceti. Believe me, you start to be real careful then. Then you really start thinking.

STYLE

You don't need an MFA in Electrical Engineering to have a good time over here in Korea, but it helps. Talk to a tart. It's like pulling a lever on a slot machine. See the cherries pop up behind her eyes every single time. This is true – there's something virginal about them, even when they're taking your money, or mine. They look crisply naked even with their Britomartian steel clothes on, which is what inviolability is all about. The one of the tarts on whom I base all my Miss Kim stabs at immortality once remarked to me: "I've been slaving away in this racket for two full epicycles of Venus, and I still don't know if I've paid off the vigorish on my last New Paradigm Shift!" "Wow," I said. "Maybe you're rigged." "What do you mean?" "Maybe the mama-san recalibrated your take while you were sleeping. Out of meanness and greed." She thought hard about this: It was a fact that in her sleep she slept the dreamless sleep of an unplugged home appliance. "You want me to check?" I said, beaming like a flashlight into a rabbithole. There were a lot of wheels and pulleys and weights down there, but no circuitry. "I don't think your cherry filling's electronic, my dear." "What are you talking about?" This was true – she was an old gravity-powered model, despite her youth. But that's Asia for you: oracle bones among the microchips. And it was breaking my heart to have to talk to her this way. She hadn't done anything illegal, herself. "You want me to rip it all out and put in a unit that lights and beeps?" She studied this offer for a while like a problem in Ptolemaic astronomy, and I guess she saw she had no real choice but to upgrade to Copernican. "*Aigo!* Will it hurt?" (*Aigo!* is the same as the Spanish *Ay de mi!* but less well known.) "Hell yes," I said. "I'm no Boy Scout." And then the fun began.

CLOSURE

One late night last week Miss Kim woke me up smack dab in the middle of the Throes – she was hemorrhaging false starts like a vending machine that has found Bejesus. Our bedclothes were soaked. She was covered with the damn starts head to toe and resembled a rock shark with a mob of remora groupies stapled to its skin. I won't even mention where the truly ugly ones had latched on. And every single one of them false as a promise. One start was spotted and smaller than the others, the runt of the litter, and kept getting kicked off its sucking place on her by the bigger ones. My heart went out to it but what can you do? You have to let nature take her course. I pinched it just behind the ears near the top of its spine, thinking nature's course would be less painful that way, and felt it shudder and convulse and expire at precisely that fatal moment printed on its underside. When all the other starts – and there were dozens of the suckers – had gotten their fill of plasma, they commenced to drop off her and roll around on the floor smacking their muzzy bellies with little tadpole boxing glove hands. Before they had a chance to shape shift back into default drool Miss Kim and I took some photographs with the intention of founding a False Start Family Album, for I knew here in Confucian Values Land starts must be nurtured carefully from the get-go, and if just one proves shamelessly false after all it is locked up in a backroom and fed through a slot. No one talks about it, let alone takes pictures of it. That's why you're unlikely to see a false start in print anywhere else save here, in the wee hours, and only smack dab in the middle of the Throes.

IMMORTALITY

Last night I met Death again, in a back alley. He is on a health kick and looks horribly warmed over. All stretched skin over cheekbones. He travels a lot by air these days and is terrified of flying. It doesn't help that the other passengers shun him. Sometimes he dresses up as an old lady and gets rip-snorting drunk on the airlines' trans-Pacific free booze and talks loud about how he once fellated Hemingway. "In the Afternoon! Ha ha ha!" (Private jokes crack him up over 30,000 feet.) But he was stone sober last night and wore a three-piece suit that he claimed had been bequeathed him by William S. Burroughs. I told him to shut the hell up because I was reading Burroughs' biography and hadn't gotten to the end yet and don't spoil it. I tried to veer him away from literature and ran smack into Aforesaid Tart with a black, squarish object hanging from her crotch by a harness of wires like a half-stolen car radio. Death started clacking his dentures and said he wanted her right now, in exactly that condition, and it became one of those ironic situations in which you find yourself protecting a woman on whom you ostensibly have no ulterior designs, a.k.a. Knightly Chivalry. At which point His Imperiousness whipped a chessboard from a sealskin portmanteau, but all the castles and bishops and paladins were little souvenir figurines of deceased rock stars: Joplin and Hendrix and Morrison and a bunch of Jerry Garcia pawns. Just as I was about to make my opening gambit, Aforesaid Tart leaned over the grid. "Yeah. Fine. Great. But where's *Elvis*? Where's the KING?" The only official Asian sighting had been a Banquo-like affair when George Bush pere collapsed into the lap of the Japanese P.M. over a platter a fugu sushi back in '91. But Aforesaid's point was well taken and Death started a Jacob (not Bob, sadly) Marley backpedal into a brick wall. I got up real close to see exactly how this sort of vanishing act was pulled off, and you know what happens? It's just like water disappearing into sand. There was an immaterial Death-shaped wet spot on that wall for weeks just like on the cover of the Who album until the local drunks pissed it into oblivion. You never know how easy it is to shake those intimidations of mortality until you take a shot at it. Of course to give Antonius Block his due, it was a lot harder way back during the Crusades when the only way to kick out the jams and really get down and boogie was a danse macabre. Later on Aforesaid Tart and I had a beer alone together. "You son of a bitching liar," she hissed. "What?" "You don't have an MFA in Electrical Engineering! Look at this damn thing dangling between my legs. I feel like a *man*!" So we went upstairs to her room and I got the unit in right like I should have done in the first place had I had the right degree. Then I wrote out a spiteful bill for "cervixes rendered" and handed it to her and told her that before 1840 all the clocks in America had wooden gears. They couldn't keep time in damp weather, but you could be damn straight they didn't go around calling other people liars either. She smiled and I looked into her eyes and I saw the cherries again. "What was your MFA *really* in, anyway – Tombstones?" "Nope. Lawn Ornaments."

LAMIA

Miss Kim crawls under our six-legger sofa and disappears for a week. I bend down in the mornings and ask her if she'd like a plate of greasy French fries or her MP3 or the new Whitesnake release, but my offer engenders no response. Sloughing, I suppose, is much like pouting, or menstruation. Occasionally I hear her shift position with a sound like crumpling cellophane. The tough part, she once remarked, was wriggling her hips through the narrow ceinture of her waist and then the slow transit out the neckhole. When I told her I *really* wanted to see that, she nearly crowned me, though perhaps she was still miffed about the afternoon I taped a souvenir maraca to her coccyx while she napped – i.e., so that when she woke up and climbed on top and arched over me she rattled like a diamondback mesmerizing prey. (This was to get her back for a crack she once made about Milking the Cobra.) She's read a book by Harry Houdini, particularly the chapter on slipping out of a straitjacket while submerged in an oversize deep-fryer, but she says she'd like to see him pull that off while crammed under a sofa with a horned foreigner coccygeaphile reaching in every five minutes to cop a feel. She nips at my fingers and I learn my lesson after a time and walk around the apartment with mercurochromed hands like Lady MacBeth. *Out, damn Spot* I snap like I'm scolding a pup, but Miss Kim doesn't budge. She goes about the real business of shedding her skin just before dawn, when she thinks I'm asleep in the other room and can't hear the hush of the audience and the drumrolls inside her head. On the seventh night the living room erupts in sudden applause and I leap out of the sack. The band strikes up and Miss Kim stands nude on the sofa taking her bows, holding up her moulted skin like a sheer suit of long-johns. The musicians shift scores to "The Stripper" and Miss

Kim acknowledges the compliment with a jaunty sequence of bumps and grinds, swinging her sheath over her head like a bolo. I settle at her feet to watch her gyrations, my hand in my lap and my hat on top of that like a 42nd Street pervert. When I come she puckers and blows me a kiss, and I get the weird, shrunken sensation I too am no longer one with my skin.

SIN

If Sir Thomas Wyatt could croak with a bulge in his tights, so may I. The only law not wholly unfathomable to me is the one against Laws. That and it's time to stop hating rich olive-throated women for spending all their vacation lives munching designer falafels in the ruined shadows of Baalbek. I'm thinking of a certain Lilith now, with a clitoris as ornery as a granary mealworm. And suddenly I might as well be dead, too, Sir Tom. Hell is a door that opens onto a wall. The music stops and you hear an eerie wailing coming from the other side. It is Eternity wearing a prayer shawl and a nose half eaten away by ceaseless gainsaying. It is time for tears and the stopping up of ears. *Where in the known world did Odysseus get the beeswax anyway?* I hear. *It was none of mine.* And then I calm down. It was only a street vendor outside, after all. But God, he sounded so *real*. I could have sworn she was standing naked in front of me like a Yeats poem. And still bitching to high heaven that I'm not on the Supreme Court and a mafia don on the side. That muff though, Miss Kim, shall remain nameless forever, like a curse even the High One is afraid to visit upon his seekers. Such is lust recollected in tranquility and one strand in the harness of clinging black tendrils that creep out of it.

ARDOR

The bogus US $100 bills being printed up in a brimstone bunker on the frosty outskirts of Pyongyang smell like winter kimchi on their inky backsides. So too with my Miss Kim and her chilly, pungent, kinky bum, though she takes this wrong and it rains pinchbeck chopsticks with our ginseng root pattern wrought on the handle-ends whenever I submit the faux analogy to her. Later taut nipples come down, but locked inside hailstones that graze my searing lips and finally pop like blanks tossed into my hectic red hammer & anvil ears. As people in general grow older and colder, their radios have to blare above their furnaces' roars. So too with plangent lovers and their planchet kisses. And the forged words we so clandestinely traffic in.

COMPETITION

I finally found a company (Rival ™) that sells electric crock pots big enough to bathe in. The ad was in the back pages of *Soldier of Fortune* magazine and when the crate arrived I had to fend off a legion of local shamans who seemed to be able to smell what was inside. Somehow they knew it was a Beauty. I had heard of guys simmering themselves in ham hocks and black-eyed peas and the babes flocking from all directions like aborigines to a Jesuit offering the Pontiff's irresistible phone number. But when I finished uncrating I realized something was amiss – the plug was as big as a boxcar coupling. The damn pots were meant for export to Mars, not Pusan, and were left over from the old Rod Serling story "To Serve Man," the part he had to cut out to make room for commercials. Due to its size I had to leave the crock part outside overnight in an empty lot beside the apartment building, and in the wee hours of the morning I heard a good hour's worth of grunting and straining and wheezy shamanesque voices whispering loudly "Hot Tub!" the way you might ejaculate "Hot Dog!" in the hoarse late innings of a tight baseball game. Let them have it, I thought. I had brought the cord and plug inside as a conversation piece, like a good neighbor unhinging the door of a junked refrigerator, so they really couldn't hurt themselves. But lately Miss Kim has become overly familiar with the thing, polishing its prongs with Bon Ami and feeding it whole shoats. I've tried to put my foot down on letting it sleep with us, but Miss Kim calls me a prude and I have to back off. She really doesn't comprehend the enormity of what it's been up to once we've slunk into slumber, but I've been examining the video footage of the nocturnal experimentations it's been performing on her for my upcoming address to the 'Patanatomists on *Eve's Dream: Eros and the Post-modern*

Home Appliance. "Ladies and Gentlemen," I expect to begin. "Submitted for your approval . ."

DECONSTRUCTION

Of a shivery Sunday afternoon Miss Kim and I climb the long spiral to my belfry so I can show her my bats. She had no idea I was almost a Superstar in my youth. Each bat has a nickname according to its exploit. My favorite is the venerable Picago Chicasso. When I bashed that damn statue in the Adam's apple, the bat barked out THERE ARE ONLY TWO KINDS OF WOMEN: GODDESSES AND DOOR-MATS among other Locker Room Vulgarities and then muttered *Perdonnez mon francais.* Miss Kim, who has HELLO tattooed on one butt cheek and GOODBYE inked in on the other like a Ouija Board with legs, lifts the stick from the bat-rack and takes a poke at me I won't repeat. "Yobo," I say. "These are the Tools of an Artist up here! Nobody's responsible for the cracks they make." I show her the pearl-handled model with which I dubbed hard Rodin's "The Kiss" one week and Brancusi's the next. Engraved along the thick part like a motto on Old Betsy: *Osculo, Ergo Sum.* Miss Kim hefts this baby and brains me on the lips. I see comic book stars and Red Crescent moons and Saturn with his love-handle rings and Miss Kim standing over me like she's Nancy Fowler Archer in *Attack of the 50 Foot Woman*. Perhaps chained galley slaves stroking their way into Rhodes Harbor gaped up at the Colossus like this. But Miss Kim is woman and the view is Divine.

AMNESIS

Miss Kim, parade-dress naked (and "naked" is one syllable to her, like "faked" or "taked"), arms swinging mechanically, marches around the apartment practicing her version of the goosestep. Lately I've been showing her Hollywood footage about World War II on our third-hand VCR, and she thinks Nazi officers were pretty slick. That there could be Good Guys and Bad Guys in a war so distant in time and space is incomprehensible to her, like a propeller-tuner trying to find work in a Jet Age. Style is everything. When I lurch out the door and slam my face into the Pusan winter wind wearing my Helot dogskin cap with its floppy earflaps, she follows at a discrete distance, Korean-wife-style, in case we run into somebody she knows, at which moment she can vanish. She says I look like Snoopy, the Trademark. I whirl around and tell her I'm a Communist bolt-action sniper tied to a tree in the mountains of the North picking off Japanese regulars like they were children on a playground. Ka-pap! Charlie Brown-san. Ka-pap! Linus-san. Ka-pap! Pig-pen-san. Ka-pap! Marcia-san. Ka-pap! Woodstock-san. Miss Kim and I step over the bodies, which are paper cut-outs shivering in the wind. Then a real gust kicks up and they blow down the street, leapfrogging each other like yesterday's newspapers, and toting away from us those names of mass murderers that so froze our blood for one moment long ago, as curiously hard to recall now as old-fashioned love, to a glacial place called Time Out Of Mind. Miss Kim and I, fully clothed, more or less together, and bloody fucking cold.

TIME

Why belabor the past? It has worked hard enough, you say. And I agree. Especially the Egyptians, who got ground down until there was nothing left but sand and about 97 million curators wandering around on it looking for canopic jars. You get a postcard from the Sphinx with only a paw-print on the message side. Too weary to write "I smell bad" or "I don't think this nose job is going to work." And the rest of history busted its balls too, digging itself so far deep down you need foundation money to call it up long distance and say you're giving it the rest of Eternity off. The past is just too tired to care. Which is why the present is better. You can walk right up to the present and say Boo! and things really start to jump. I taught this trick to Miss Kim and she caught on fast. She said Boo! to our cactus and it made breakfast. She said Boo! to my coccyx and I was up for days, mutating. By the time I got back from the future and had seen what that was all about, I was an unchanged man. I mean the future really works, and hard. Of course, it is full of coccyx-less robots who get nervous if they have to take lunchbreaks. They see the sushi vending machines slaving away for small change and tell themselves they can't really be hungry. The factories of the future are humming, but they don't know any words. I think I'll just stay back here at this punctiform moment in temporality with Miss Kim and play.

PROPINQUITY

Someone once said that God created the moon to titillate the multitudes in each one of us. When that got old he created miniature golf under the lights. The idea was to keep a pock-marked sphere in front of our eyes. That is, we're destined for Outer Space but we'll never get there in time. There are radios blaring all over the Cosmos and the place is lit up like a free-for-all Saturday Night. But nobody can go out because the air doesn't work. We sit around the pad and yak at each other in tv screen Exilese. Then something trips over a tricycle out in the hall. They're out there! They made it! A superior Race! Miss Kim squats down by the door so I can peer through her slot, which is curved like a time-warp but adjustable by hand. Mimicking twin eternal Dark Ages dying to expire, we wait for her knockers to chime. Then the ear-oil phone rings. We answer. It's Herm down the hall. "Don't open your door. I can see them from here. It's the Zeuses in gas masks and zoot suits, and they brought their damn kids."

LOSS

That drumming you hear is my blood beating its elbows inside my temples so that I feel like I'm trying to sprout a new set of horns. I bee-line to the bathroom to see if I can catch what my mug is up to, but Miss Kim has borrowed the Eveready AA's again that give the mirror its power to Reflect Upon Life. I push my crest back up to where it has fallen from and work my jaw around to see if I have been punched. And suddenly the acid I dropped back in Real Time kicks in. Either that or I've been tripping for eons and only now just crashed. At any rate, it is just The Same Old Knowledge Of Reality. Miss Kim never existed. I've been slapping my own ass for months and squealing like a girl. I guess I got so good at it that other people saw her too, standing there next to me like one of the fabled Soong Sisters with vents up to her armpits and nothing on underneath. Except the pair of AA's she slips under her tarsals and which give her the gait of a float in a parade. "Mom, look at her!" the neighborhood kids holler in pure puer Korean. "Her feet's not touching the ground!" She never really gets all that high up but kids are low and notice things we consider beneath us. Then I hear the drone of the little hovercraft propellers on the soles of her slippers. She's back! And I thought I'd lost her! She massages my temples with Tiger Balm and the elbows stop their racket. "Where were you?" I ask, and she leans over and deposits the slithery AA's like oil-drum eggs in the cupped palms of my mendicant hands: "Getting ready to be ready to be here."

TRUTH

A hiccup is the dog inside you trying to get out, I tell Miss Kim. She nods sagely and goes back to nibbling my coccyx. No practitioners of Timeless Asian Sex, we invented this one ourselves and it feels good, the way each leap in evolution must have felt a little bit better, each shortening of the tail and each tender new knob on the skull. And I am evolving, a secret I let out only when I gape in the mirror. The mirror gapes right back and says things like You Find Your Niche And You Fill It and other conundrums. Once it even spoke in something like verse: Tapyr Tapyr Burning Bright In The Florists Of The Night. I corrected its spelling and it would not speak to me for half a year. During this respite I began to read seriously. The instruction booklet that came with my coffee pot was especially engrossing. Now I understood exactly *why* it did not enjoy being immersed in water. I had always thought it was a religious thing, a matter of principle. You grow and you learn. Meanwhile, during all of this, Miss Kim continues to gnaw and I sail blithely toward Enlightenment or Oblivion, whichever comes first. From the instruction booklet I leapt directly to Sumerian clay cylinders. But whether you read up and down or spin them like a dowel I haven't figured out yet. The tiny filaments embedded in the gray cardboard core of a roll of toilet paper may contain the secrets of the universe, if only you look hard enough. And, oh, Miss Kim, the beauty of the terror is that some things never get old.

ACKNOWLEDGMENTS

Poems and prose poems in this collection originally appeared as follows:
"Six Footnotes to the Buddha's Birthday"
"Down Letter Home to a Poet Friend"
"4:40 A.M. Anonymous Phone Call" *Exquisite Corpse*
"Sarge: By Way of Introduction"
"Recognition"
"Poetry Too Has Its Role to Play, He Insisted" *Foreign Literary Journal*
"An Angel Of English" *Ceciles Writers*
"Korean Rock Garden" *Tomorrow Magazine*
"Recovery" *Rain Dog Review*
"Pusan Raindrop Pusan Woman" (Part 1 only) *Chikyu* (Tokyo)
"Pusan Raindrop Pusan Woman" (Part 3 only) *Rat's Ass Review*
"On His Fabled Generosity; Or, Her American Dream" *Blank Gun Silencer*
"In English the Korean Word *BOP* Means 'Glutinous Rice'; Or, At the Women's College" *Libido*
"On Bumping into a Formerly Snaggle-Toothed Young Neighbor" *The Atticus Review*
"Drill"
"Divinations" *Slipstream*
"Miss Min's Magic Monday Morning" *Cha Magazine* (Hong Kong)
"Zen Detective Exam Question #38" *Spillway*
"A Visitor"
"Bachelor Stripped Bare by His Housewives, Even" *Pearl*
"A Tale of Two Peninsulas" *Watching the Perseids: The Backwaters Press Twentieth Anniversary Anthology*
"In a Station of the Metro" *Carbon Culture Review*
"ESL Teacher"
"The Gentle Monk: A Fire Sermon"
"Ardor"
"The Sleeping Beauties" *Fluid in Darkness, Frozen in Light* (Poetry Collection, Pearl Editions, Long Beach). The book is now out of print and all rights belong to the author.

"Propinquity"
"Time"
"Truth"
"Sin"
"Gillagain"   *The Prose Poem: An International Journal*
"Deconstruction"   *Apalachee Quarterly*
"Deregulation"
"Pen(w(o))manship"
"Technique"
"Introduction to Universal Psychophonetics: The B's"   *Quarter After Eight*
"Integration"   *Amaranth*
"Chinoiserie"   *XIB*
"Lamia"   *Maverick*
"Class"
"Domesticity"   *First Intensity*
"Transparence"   *Juxta*
"Fate"   *key satch(el)*
"Art"
"Loss"   *Lightning & Ash*
"Identity"   *Left Bank Review*
"Immortality"   *Nebo*
"Amnesis"   *Pavement Saw*

The prose poems in the "B's Chorea: A Poet's Journal" section were excerpted from the metafictional flash novella *Perchan's Chorea: Eros and Exile* (Watermark Press, Wichita). The book is now out of print and all rights belong to the author.

ROBERT J. PERCHAN: PUBLICATIONS

Overdressed to Kill (Poetry) . . Backwaters Press (Omaha, 2006) Winner of the 2005 Weldon Kees Poetry Chapbook Award

Mythic Instinct Afternoon (Poetry) . . Poetry West (Boulder, 2005) Winner of the 2005 Poetry West Chapbook Award

A Foreign Student's Guide to Three Classic American Modern Novels: Fitzgerald's The Great Gatsby, *Hemingway's* The Sun Also Rises, *and Faulkner's* Light in August . . Hyung Seul Publishers (Seoul, Korea, 2003)

Fluid in Darkness, Frozen in Light (Poetry) . . Pearl Editions (Long Beach, California, 2000) Winner of the 1999 Pearl Poetry Prize

Perchan's Chorea: Eros and Exile (Fiction) . . Watermark Press (Wichita, Kansas, 1991) Translated into French by Valerie Morlot as *La Choree de Perchan (eros et exil)* and published by Quidam Editeur (Meudon, France, 2002)

Robert Perchan was born in Cleveland, Ohio, and grew up there doing pretty much what was expected of him. After grad school he taught introductory composition and literature courses for the U.S. Navy's Program for Afloat College Education (PACE) on ships deployed in Rota, Spain, the Mediterranean Sea and the Western Pacific Ocean before settling into a life of reflective if occasionally perplexed peninsularity. For many years he taught British and American literature at universities in South Korea while contributing numerous essays, stories and poems to literary journals (*Exquisite Corpse* and *The Prose Poem: An International Journal* among many others) and anthologies both in the USA and abroad. His poetry collection *Fluid in Darkness, Frozen in Light* won the 1999 Pearl Poetry Prize and the final judge, after generously praising the poems therein, was perspicacious enough to offer this prophetic observation about the author on the back cover: "I suspect he will not be invited to the White House for Poetry Month celebrations . . ." That was like about five Presidents ago, and thankfully appears to be holding true. In any case, Bob continues to eat and drink and write in Busan, South Korea, under the bemused gaze of his wife, Mi-kyung Lee, who has done the real work over the past several years translating novels by Jane Austen, Elizabeth Gaskell and Sinclair Lewis.

Photo by Mi-kyung Lee